The Mediating Self

The Mediating Self

Mead, Sartre, and Self-Determination

MITCHELL ABOULAFIA

Yale University Press
New Haven and London

Designed by Christopher Harris
and set in Sabon type
by Graphic Composition, Inc.
Printed in the United States of America by
Edwards Brothers, Inc., Ann Arbor, Michigan

Library of Congress Cataloging-in-Publication Data

Aboulafia, Mitchell,
    The mediating self.

    Bibliography: p.
    Includes index.
    1. Mead, George Herbert, 1863–1931. 2. Sartre,
Jean-Paul, 1905–1980. 3. Free will and determinism—
History—20th century. 4. Self (Philosophy)—History—20th
century. 5. Social psychology—History—
20th century. I. Title.
B945.M464A63   1986   123'.5   85-20378
ISBN 0-300-03523-5 (cloth)
ISBN 0-300-05479-9 (pbk.)

The paper in this book meets the guidelines for permanence
and durability of the Committee on Production Guidelines
for Book Longevity of the Council on Library Resources.

10   9   8   7   6   5   4   3   2

For
Barbara Ellman
who transforms through recognition

Contents

ACKNOWLEDGMENTS ix

INTRODUCTION xiii

PART I

CHAPTER ONE. *G. H. Mead*
Sociality and the Object Self 3

CHAPTER TWO. *Sartre*
Consciousness, Self, and the Other 27

CHAPTER THREE. *Mead and Sartre*
Comparison and Critique 45

PART II

CHAPTER FOUR. *From Mediated to Mediating Self*
The Development of the Self-
Determining Self 73

CHAPTER FIVE. *The Circumscribed Self*
Domination and Self-Determination 102

BIBLIOGRAPHY 127

INDEX 133

Acknowledgments

<small>THERE IS AN INHERENT TENSION IN ACKNOWLEDGMENTS PAGES</small> that I have not been able to resolve. The page is by its nature a rather standardized one, appearing in the most diverse books and presenting more or less the same information with different names inserted. I wish, as I am sure most writers must, not only to have my book recognized as a unique and worthy contribution, but to have those who were and are important to me and my work acknowledged in an appropriate manner. The eloquence required for such a task, even if I possessed it, would not be suitable to an acknowledgments page.

I can now see that I had been writing this work long before I had written a word or outlined a chapter. I cannot possibly thank all of those who have been of assistance through so many years, but I do want to make some attempt. For intellectual and moral support I would like to thank Matthew Aboulafia, Oliva Blanchette, Joe Esposito, John Gorman, Carol Gould, Patrick Heelan, Mark Kulstad, George Lipsitz, Craig Oettinger, Donald Quataert, Jean Quataert, and Marx Wartofsky. For reading early versions of the manuscript and making helpful comments: Thomas Blakeley, Steven Crowell, David L. Miller, Elliot Pruzan, Mitchell Smolkin, and Mark Tish. Nor can I fail to mention my students at UH-Clear Lake, especially those in the various graduate seminars I have offered the last few years, who have shared their enthusiasm and questions. I thank Richard Grandy and the philosophy department of Rice University for making an outsider feel at home on so many occasions. I also want to thank Pam Sisk and Margaret Simpson for typing assistance. Jeanne Ferris, the philosophy and psychology editor at Yale, and Jean van Altena, manuscript editor, were not only exceedingly helpful, but were a pleasure to work with. And I thank Lauren Ellman Aboulafia, without whose presence this study would have been finished at an earlier date, while surely being all the poorer for it. Besides, though she will not be able to read this book for a number of years, I promised I would put her name in it.

The Melrose-Thompson Fund of the University of Houston-Clear Lake was kind enough to supply me with a summer stipend in 1983, during which time I was able to accomplish a good deal of research and writing. I would like to thank the Office of Vice Chancellor and Provost Charles Hardwick for a stipend during the summer of 1984. Several publishers have been kind enough to grant me permission to cite from their copyrighted works and I would like to thank them for so doing.

Allen & Unwin, for Hegel's *Science of Logic,* trans. A. V. Miller, copyright, 1969.

Hogarth Press, for rights to *The Complete Psychological Works of Sigmund Freud* outside the U.S.A., its territories, and the Philippines.

Methuen & Co., for rights to Sartre's *Being and Nothingness* outside of the U.S.A. and Canada.

W. W. Norton, for Freud's *Civilization and its Discontents,* copyright 1961 by James Strachey; and *Group Psychology and the Analysis of the Ego,* copyright 1959 by Sigmund Freud Copyrights LTD. and James Strachey.

Open Court, for *The Philosophy of Jean-Paul Sartre,* edited by Paul Arthur Schilpp, copyright 1981 by *The Library of Living Philosophers.*

Oxford University Press, for Hegel's *Phenomenology of Spirit,* trans. A. V. Miller, copyright 1977; and Hegel's *Philosophy of Nature,* trans. A. V. Miller, copyright 1970.

Philosophical Library, for Sartre's *Being and Nothingness,* trans. Hazel E. Barnes, copyright 1956.

University of Chicago Press, for G. H. Mead's *Mind, Self, and Society,* edited by Charles W. Morris, copyright 1934; *Philosophy of the Act,* edited by Charles W. Morris, copyright 1938; *The Phi-*

losophy of the Present, edited by Arthur E. Murphy, copyright 1932 by Open Court Publishing Co., Phoenix Edition 1980; *Selected Writings,* copyright 1964 by Andrew J. Reck, Phoenix edition 1981; and David L. Miller's *George Herbert Mead: Self, Language, and the World,* copyright 1973 by David L. Miller, Phoenix Edition 1980.

Finally, I should like to note that portions of chapters 1, 2, and 3 have appeared in my article "Mead, Sartre: Self, Object, and Reflection," *Philosophy and Social Criticism,* volume 11, no. 2.

Introduction

I ORIGINALLY INTENDED TO SUBTITLE THIS WORK "A SOCIOLOGY of freedom" but subsequently abandoned the idea on account of the intolerable ambiguity of the phrase. *Freedom* is difficult enough to define, and *sociology* brings to mind everything from Gallup polls to the musings of the Frankfurt school. Moreover, this book is intended as a philosophical work, although some may see it as falling more in the realm of speculative psychology, or metapsychology. Nevertheless, I cannot help but think that the phrase "sociology of freedom" says something important in terms of its content.

For quite some time now, I have been concerned with what is meant by the term *self,* and to what extent it is determined. Claiming, as I am inclined to do, that the self is both determined and free raises classical philosophical questions, questions that are no less difficult in their modern context. The history of Western thought is not, of course, without numerous writers who have sought to characterize the self for which freedom is possible. In our times, however, influential assertions regarding the importance of socialization in the development of the self mark an unprecedented challenge to affirmations of individual autonomy and freedom of existential choice. In light of these assertions, how are we to understand a self that (seemingly) has the rather astounding capacity to transform and determine itself? The contemporary challenge, as I see it, is to reconcile the apparent truths of modern psychology and sociology—which entail, by and large, deterministic assumptions and conclusions—with the experience of individual autonomy and self-determination. Part One of this book studies these contrasting positions, and Part Two attempts to bring them together.

The figures chosen to act as representatives of the two approaches are George Herbert Mead and Jean-Paul Sartre, not only because of the originality of their work, but also because of the unique character of their thought, which encompasses many themes found in twentieth-century philosophy, psychology, and sociology. I am convinced that both Mead—pragmatist, neo-Hegelian, booster of scientific method, inventor of such widely employed sociological concepts as "taking the role of the other" and the "generalized other," defender of the self as a social object—and the early Sartre of *Transcendence of the Ego* and *Being and Nothingness*—existentialist, defender of the spontaneous, opponent of determinism and scientism, critic of those who wish to reduce the self and consciousness to mere objects of psychological investigation—are thinkers that must be reckoned with if one is to grasp the nature of the self and self-determination. To be more specific, Mead is unique in his discernment regarding the genesis of reflective consciousness, in which the self is seen as a social object first and foremost, whereas Sartre is quite sensitive to the dimension of noncognitive, pre-reflective experience and provides penetrating accounts of existential choice. On the other hand, Mead, though he addresses the question of the spontaneity of the individual, is not attuned to the individual's pre-reflective experience, because he bifurcates consciousness into non-reflective and reflective spheres, and Sartre's attempts to account for the relationship between reflective consciousness and pre-reflective consciousness are inadequate, due in part to a dependence on what might be termed his novel brand of literary psychologism. The Mead of *Mind, Self, and Society* and *The Philosophy of the Present* and the early Sartre of *Transcendence of the Ego* and *Being and Nothingness* provide an excellent study in contrast, not of irreconcilable opposites, but of two sides of a coin, both of which are necessary to the whole.

This work is not solely a study of Mead and Sartre, however. In order to reconcile their contrasting positions and provide an account of self and self-determination, additional viewpoints and concepts are necessary—Hegel's concept of limit and his dialectic of master and slave, for example, and Freud's views on identification and introjection. This essay, then, attempts to provide an account of the self and its development with reference to these thinkers, in order to articulate how the capacity for self-determination arises. It should by no means be regarded as an attempt at a comprehensive analysis of child development, for there are far too many aspects of this development to be explored in one work. The focus here is on those facets of development that give rise to what, following Sartre, I call a "sense of self," which is what makes self-determination possible. One may view this work as integrating certain features of the existential approach to freedom and selfhood with a social psychological account of the self, an account which sees the self as constituted in symbolic social interaction.

The first two chapters are expository and allow Mead and Sartre to speak for themselves on consciousness, self-consciousness, and intersubjectivity, and on the relationship of these topics to the development and nature of the self. The third chapter offers a comparative analysis of Mead and Sartre which articulates the limitations of each. The fourth offers a "solution" to the problems posed in the third, by presenting an original answer to the question How is self-determination possible? The last chapter discusses the importance of recognition in the realization of the self-determining self and examines the way in which relationships of domination prevent the development of the self.

To the extent that it argues that self-determination emerges from social experience, the work is a sociology of freedom. This is to say not only that freedom of choice depends on a social context for its realization (one could not choose to be a symphony conductor before orchestras came into existence), but that the consciousness which allows for self-determination is itself constituted in and through the social. The issue is a difficult one, for it seems that if one is constituted by the social, one becomes merely a microcosm of the social, a thoroughly socialized being, in which case self-determination can only mean reconciling oneself to the given order, an order which implies a social version of the determinism of Spinoza, leading to the intellectual love of society as a possible method of reconciliation. However, this is not what we usually mean by self-determination, for if self-determination means anything at all, it implies that one can actively depart from prevailing norms and expectations in the process of selecting (new) values, and that one can act in a manner commensurate with one's own (changing) values, desires, and tastes. While I would not want this to stand as an all-encompassing definition of *self-determination,* it does point to a crucial element in the meaning of the term as it will be used in this work: one is not merely determined and constituted by the other but can consciously transform oneself. The capacity for self-determination comes about not in spite of, but rather because of, the peculiar nature of the self's social development. Unlike many accounts which set so-called individual freedom and social determinism irreconcilably at odds, I will argue that what is often located at the heart of individual freedom, the capacity to decide in a purposeful fashion what one believes or what course of action to follow, is itself to be understood as integrally bound to the social. My aim, then, is to show how the mediated self, the self that becomes what it is through its relationships with others, becomes the mediating self, the self that can determine the direction of its own life.

To accomplish this task I will rely on Mead's concept of *sociality.* For Mead, the self is a system of social relations, a system that undergoes alteration and change due to interaction with novel events. Sociality is the conceptual device Mead employs to understand how the self can be both a fixed system of social relations and a system that is transformed through its association with others. In order to augment Mead's account of the self as an open, but non-self-determining, system, I will adopt a position held by many existentialists, namely, that consciousness (or the self) is free by virtue of being aware of its possibilities, of what it lacks, or of its privations. I will argue, however, that the lack of which we are aware is not a given of human nature or of consciousness but arises in response to certain forms of social interaction. I thus challenge the Sartrean claim that pre-reflective (self-) consciousness is prior to, and more fundamental than, reflective consciousness.

Finally, this work concentrates on how it is possible for self-determination to arise by specifying certain crucial features of the self's development. Clearly, some socioeconomic systems promote features that catalyze this self, whereas others do not. Nevertheless, aside from one very brief discussion of how the present Western market economy can act to hinder the development of this self, I do not discuss the merits of various socioeconomic systems with regard to the development of the self, not because the subject is unimportant, but because it deserves to be treated in a separate work.

The Mediating Self

Part I

CHAPTER ONE

G. H. Mead

Sociality and the Object Self

IN AN INTERVIEW OF 1975 JEAN-PAUL SARTRE STATED THAT IN HIS early years he thought that "philosophy ultimately meant psychology," a psychology especially concerned with the life of consciousness.[1] George Herbert Mead's close friend John Dewey wrote in his prefatory remarks to Mead's *Philosophy of the Present:* "When I first came to know Mr. Mead, well over forty years ago, the dominant problem in his mind concerned the nature of consciousness as personal and private."[2] In contrast to Sartre, Mead's interest in consciousness led him not in the direction of phenomenological description, but on a quest to understand and account for the development of mind and self-consciousness.

Mead came to argue that mind, self, and self-consciousness arise and develop as a result of linguistic, or symbolic, interaction. As a "product" of this interaction, the self has a genesis that can be observed and studied scientifically, and research reveals that the self and reflective self-consciousness originate together in non-reflective experience. For Mead, there is no self without self-consciousness, and self-consciousness (reflection) does not come into being until there is language. An infant's experience is thus non-reflective. However, Mead views non-reflective experience not only as a fundamental feature of infancy and the original ground of reflection,

---

1. Jean-Paul Sartre, "An Interview with Jean-Paul Sartre," in *The Philosophy of Jean-Paul Sartre,* Library of the Living Philosophers, vol. 16, p. 8; hereafter referred to as "The Interview."

2. George Herbert Mead, *The Philosophy of the Present,* p. xxxvi; hereafter referred to as *PP.*

but as the companion of reflective self-consciousness throughout life. In the words of David L. Miller: "Experience, then, includes more than that of which we are aware. Reflective acts, cognition, reference, and awareness arise within a *world that is there,* experienced in its immediacy."[3] And Mead writes:

This immediate experience which is reality, and which is the final test of the reality of scientific hypotheses as well as the test of the truth of all our ideas and suppositions, is the experience of what I have called the "biologic individual." . . . [This] term lays emphasis on the living reality which may be distinguished from reflection. . . . [A]ctual experience did not take place in this form but in the form of unsophisticated reality.[4]

Reserving comparative analysis for chapter 3, I will not pause here to comment on the implications of the above statements for Sartre's existentialism. Instead, I will proceed to the question at hand: How do mind, self, and self-consciousness develop from non-reflective, non-cognitive experience? It is worth noting in passing, however, that the manner in which the term *reflection* is used in the above passages suggests the intimate connection between the reflective quality of self-consciousness, consciousness as that which reflects on itself as an object, and the mental operation, or process, we think of when we speak of reflecting on a problem, that is, reasoning. For Mead, cognition and self-consciousness are linked and are set over and against the non-reflective "world that is there." The existential realm of the immediate cannot be denied: it is the ground upon which science must stand even in its most abstruse reflective ruminations. Nonetheless, Mead is not an existentialist.

He thought of himself as a pragmatist, but his indebtedness to the idealism of Hegel and Royce (one of his teachers at Harvard) is readily apparent. The label most often appended to his name is social behaviorist, though it does not allow for the non-behavioral aspects of his position. Although he sought a behavioristic explanation of the genesis of the self, of mind, he was dissatisfied with the reductionism of a John B. Watson. "The behaviorism which we

3. David L. Miller, *George Herbert Mead: Self, Language, and the World,* p. 37; emphasis added.

4. George Herbert Mead, *Mind, Self, and Society,* pp. 352–53; hereafter referred to as *MSS.*

shall make use of ... is simply an approach to the study of the experience of the individual from the point of view of his conduct, particularly, but not exclusively, the conduct as it is observable by others" (MSS, p. 2).

Introspective psychology cannot be scientific. Yet this does not mean that many of its categories—for example, mind, consciousness—are simply reducible to behaviors that others observe. We can study conduct, behavior, in order to see how features traditionally associated with mind arise, emerge from non-cognitive experience. Study of this sort reveals the importance in the development of mind of gesture. "The term 'gesture' may be identified with these beginnings of social acts which are stimuli for the response of other [living] forms" (MSS, p. 43).

Mead illustrates what he means by a gesture, which he also refers to as a "truncated act," through what he calls the conversation of gestures that we find in a fight between dogs. Each dog has learned that a gesture of a certain type—snarling, for example—is likely to be followed by certain behaviors; hence the dog that is snarled at responds in an appropriate fashion—for example, by snarling back. He does this before the other dog moves to the next "stage" of the act and bites him because no defense is shown. The gesture is, then, a way to "embody" a set of behaviors, and we may think of an entire set of behaviors as an act. A gesture, as part of an act, comes to stand for an entire (possible) act; hence, Mead also thinks of a gesture as a truncated act. A conversation of gestures is possible when each organism can "anticipate" what a specific gesture stands for—for example, that a snarl precedes and suggests attack.

Gestures of this sort appear to be common to many animals. What is it, then, about the way in which human beings interact which sets their gestures apart from those of other animals? It is that human beings are capable of gestures which Mead calls "significant symbols." "Gestures become significant symbols when they implicitly arouse in an individual making them the same responses which they explicitly arouse, or are supposed to arouse, in other individuals" (MSS, p. 47). In other words, a gesture comes to mean the same thing to one individual as it does to another. So, to use Mead's example, if I shake my fist at you, you assume not only that I am angry but that I have "some idea behind it. You assume that it means not only a possible attack, but that the individual has an idea in his experience" (p. 45). The dog who snarls is not conscious of the meaning of his snarl; he cannot scare himself but instead scares the other dog. On the other hand, it is conceivable that I could scare myself, as well as the other, when using a significant symbol that is meant to scare, because the symbol means the same to me as to the other, and each of us is aware of its meaning at the same time. If I scream at you to watch out as you step off a curb just as an unexpected car turns the corner, I can feel myself tending to jump out of the way also. In other words, I heed my own yell, my own symbol. But how can significant symbols arise from animal gestures, where the gesture means only what the other animal is going to do in response (for example, the growl of a dog simply means the other dog's response of running or fighting)?[5]

Speech is the key that allows for a very special relationship to words acting as symbols. "In the case of the vocal gesture the form [the organism] hears its own stimulus just as when this is used by other forms, so it tends to respond also to its own stimulus as it responds to the stimulus of other forms" (*MSS*, p. 65).

If I possess no significant symbols and look threateningly at you, you will respond. But unless I look in a mirror, I will not be able to respond to myself, to my own stimulus. With a vocal gesture I can hear myself as others hear me, and I can respond to my gesture as others respond. Mead is well aware of the fact that the hearing of a vocal gesture presupposes a sufficiently sophisticated nervous system, and that infants are born with the potential for this ability as a result of the evolutionary development of the species, a development in which the manipulation of objects by the hand played a key role. Mead is a theorist of the evolutionary process, as well as of the social constitution of the self, and he is a defender of the concept of emergence (which I will discuss below). "Language . . . would not have emerged had not the hands been freed from supporting the body and capable, through the juxtaposition of the thumb and the fingers, of dissecting and reassembling objects."[6] Yet

5. "The mechanism of meaning is thus present in the social act before the emergence of consciousness or awareness of meaning occurs. The act or adjustive response of the second organism gives to the gesture of the first organism the meaning which it has" (*MSS*, p. 77–78).

6. Miller, *George Herbert Mead*, p. 62. I do not interpret Mead (or Miller on Mead) to be precluding the possibility of a sophisticated hand sign language, but only to be emphasizing the unique and critical importance of the verbal gesture.

the vocal gesture, and not the movement of the hands, "is the basic gesture which does influence the individual as it influences others" (*MSS*, p. 68).

We continually elicit responses in others, and as we do so, we implicitly respond ourselves, for we hear what the other hears. "The critical importance of language in the development of human experience lies in this fact that the stimulus is one that can react upon the speaking individual as it reacts upon the other" (p. 69). An uncomplicated example of this would be when I command someone else to open a door; if he or she does not respond fast enough to my command, the tendency in myself to open the door, which has become aroused by my own command to the other, becomes heightened. I might even find myself moving toward the door to carry out my own command. Of course, there can be a variety of responses to a specific vocal gesture, depending on context, for example, but what makes a vocal gesture a significant symbol is that it tends to call out similar responses in myself and the other, the similarity being of a functional nature. "Mead contends that the meaning of sameness or similarity is derived from the functional identity of responses; that if two different particulars answer to functionally identical responses (the universal), then they are said to be similar or the same."[7]

The significant symbol differs from the gesture in that it entails self-consciousness, and self-consciousness in this context is defined as an awareness of meaning. Meaning exists in a social act, whether it is performed by a human being or by a member of another species. A dog growls, and another dog flees, the meaning of the growl being given in the second dog's response of fleeing. In this sense meaning is not a mental phenomenon but exists objectively in the field of experience. It exists for nonhuman consciousness, as well as for human consciousness that is not self-conscious. On the other hand, only on the level of self-consciousness does a symbol function as a *significant* symbol. "Gestures may be either conscious (significant) or unconscious (non-significant). The conversation of gestures is not significant below the human level, because it is not conscious, that is, not *self*-conscious (though it is conscious in the sense of involving feelings or sensations)" (*MSS*, p. 81).

In the above passage Mead distinguishes between self-conscious-

7. Ibid., p. 13.

ness, which deals with significant symbols, and consciousness, which entails feelings and sensations. At other times he uses the term *consciousness* to suggest "the environment of the human individual or social group in so far as constituted by or dependent upon or existentially relative to that individual or social group" (pp. 111–12). However, the consciousness that is aware of meanings does not simply have an environment within which it acts; it is aware of meanings in this particular environment; it is self-conscious. For consciousness of meaning to exist, a symbol must evoke the same (functional) response in me as it does in the other. Only when significant symbols exist can we speak of mind.

Mentality on our approach simply comes in when the organism is able to point out meanings to others and to himself. This is the point at which mind appears, or if you like, emerges. . . . It is absurd to look at the mind simply from the standpoint of the individual human organism; for, although it has its focus there, it is essentially a social phenomenon; even its biological functions are primarily social. [pp. 132–33]

If I did not implicitly respond as the other responds to my gesture, I would never develop mind. But because I do respond (implicitly) to my vocal gesture as the other responds, I come to take the attitude of the other toward myself by becoming aware of the meaning of my gesture, the response that my gesture evokes in the other. In so doing I develop a reflective consciousness. I view my gesture from the perspective of the other, which at first is merely the perspective of the single response of the other but later becomes the complex set of responses known as a role.

It is by means of reflexiveness—the turning-back of the experience of the individual upon himself—that the whole social process is thus brought into the experience of the individuals involved in it; it is by such means, which enable the individual to take the attitude of the other toward himself, that the individual is able consciously to adjust himself to that process. . . . Reflexiveness, then, is the essential condition, within the social process, for the development of mind. [p. 134]

I "see" myself—that is, my gestures—as others see me; I become an object to myself as I respond to my own gestures as if I were the other. Through play, children learn not only to make the specific responses of others (to their gestures) their own, they also learn to make a complex set of responses, the role of the other, their own. Animals play, but only human beings play at being someone else; the child plays at being mom or dad, for example, by taking care of his or her baby doll, and is rewarded for so doing. The child uses a complex set of gestures as the other does and learns to respond as the other would. Eventually the child comes not only to address dolls and other children from the perspective of certain roles—for example, mom, dad, teacher, or doctor—but to play at being doctor by responding to him or herself in the role of patient. In other words, the child learns how to play at, and be, both subject and object. "The child says something in one character and responds in another character, and then his responding in another character is a stimulus to himself in the first character, and so the conversation goes on" (p. 151). This rudimentary process of being subject and object, which is necessary for self-consciousness to arise, entails temporality. One cannot play both roles at once, cannot be both subject and object at the same moment; hence, Mead claims, a temporal lag is involved. Mead does not subscribe to the notion that consciousness can have an immediate (direct) awareness of itself or an immediate awareness of an ego that is aware; the consciousness that proves to be aware of "self" is not the "self" of which it is aware. We will return to the importance of temporality below, but first we must examine one of Mead's most important concepts.

In their play, children (and adults for that matter) may do more than simply take the roles of specific others. They may also engage in organized games, which involve interactions between several participants that are governed by certain rules. Mead's favorite example is baseball, which requires that one be prepared to take various roles, and be able to relate these roles to one another. If I am to play second base, I must be familiar with all the other positions since I must know what the other players are going to do. I must be able to see the game as a whole "What he [the baseball player] does is controlled by his being everyone else on that team, at least in so far as those attitudes affect his own particular response. We get then an 'other' which is an organization of the attitudes of those involved in the same process" (p. 154).

In such situations the child no longer responds to a specific other but to the roles of various others which are unified into a whole;

and the rules of the game are employed to clarify and define the attitudes of the participants.[8] Though Mead uses the example of a game, it is important to keep in mind that what he is really talking about is any organized set of responses which can be viewed as a system. So, for example, if we think of a family as a system, as various mutually interdependent roles which guide, and are guided by, implicit or explicit rules of interaction, we have "an organization of the attitudes of those involved." The other when so organized is referred to as "a" or "the generalized other," one of Mead's most noteworthy neologisms.

The organized community or social group which gives to the individual his unity of self may be called "the generalized other." The attitude of the generalized other is the attitude of the whole community. Thus, for example, in the case of such a social group as a ball team, the team is the generalized other in so far as it enters—as an organized process or social activity—into the experience of any one of the individual members of it. [p. 154; emphasis added]

Note that in the above passage the generalized other is responsible for the self's unity. What, then, is the self which is being unified in this manner?

For Mead there is no self without self-consciousness. A self cannot arise in a creature without the capacity to be both subject and object to itself. The self, by definition, is a phenemenon of reflection, dependent upon the significant symbol, upon sociality, upon being able to take the role of the other.

And he becomes a self in his experience only insofar as one attitude on his own part calls out the corresponding attitude in the social undertaking.

This is just what we imply in "self-consciousness." We appear as selves in our conduct insofar as we ourselves take the attitude that others take

---

8. "In the game, then, there is a set of responses of such others so organized that the attitude of one calls out the appropriate attitudes of the other. This organization is put in the form of the rules of the game. Children take a great interest in rules. They make rules on the spot in order to help themselves out of difficulties. . . . Now, the rules are the set of responses which a particular attitude calls out" (*MSS,* pp. 151–52).

toward us, in these correlative activities. . . . We take the role of . . . the "generalized other." And in doing this we appear as social objects, as selves.[9]

Clearly, the self here is not a soul, a substance, or a transcendental ego. We become selves by becoming objects to ourselves, and we do this by taking the attitude of the other to ourselves. I begin to act in a certain manner, I view the action from the perspective of the other, and the original (tendency to) act is then seen as (an aspect of) myself. This process will be further clarified when we look at Mead's distinction between the "I" and the "me." Here it is worth noting the complexity of the self, for it is not only in relation to specific others that we become object-selves, but in relation to the generalized other which "embodies" the collective attitudes of a society or group, and whose role we are constantly taking toward ourselves. The self begins as behaviors, behaviors that become roles, roles that we become aware of taking by viewing them from the perspective of the other. This burgeoning self eventually comes to be seen from the perspective of the generalized other, but only after we have internalized the complex of attitudes that go to make up our social environment. I do not merely *watch* myself from the perspective of the generalized other; I see myself from this perspective as it orders and frames the behaviors which I view as myself. The unity of a self, then, is made possible by the presence of the "organizing" generalized other; without it one would be no more than an unintegrated set of responses to specific others, a series of unintegrated roles.

So the self reaches its full development by organizing these individual attitudes of others into the organized social or group attitudes, and by thus becoming an individual reflection of the general systematic pattern of social or group behavior in which it and the others are all involved—a pat-

9. George Herbert Mead, "The Genesis of the Self and Social Control," in *Selected Writings,* p. 284. In *MSS* Mead states that "self-consciousness, rather than affective experience with its motor accompaniments, provides the core and primary structure of the self. . . . The essence of the self, as we have said, is cognitive: it lies in the internalized conversation of gestures which constitutes thinking, or in terms of which thought or reflection proceeds. And hence the origin and foundations of the self, like those of thinking, are social" (p. 173).

tern which enters as a whole into the individual's experience in terms of these organized group attitudes which, through the mechanism of his central nervous system, he takes toward himself, just as he takes the individual attitudes of others. [*MSS*, p. 158]

Mead goes on to tell us that a person's character is found in the capacity to take the role of the (or a) generalized other, to make the attitudes of a community one's own.[10] We should not look to idiosyncratic personal habits for character but to "a structure of attitudes . . . which goes to make up a self" (p. 163). Many habits are never brought to self-consciousness, but it is in self-consciousness that we find "an awakening in ourselves of the group of attitudes which we are arousing in others. . . . Consciousness, as frequently used, simply has reference to the field of experience, but self-consciousness refers to the ability to call out in ourselves a set of definite responses which belong to the others of the group" (p. 163).

But if "the structure of his self expresses or reflects the general behavior pattern of this social group to which he belongs" (p. 164), how are we to understand Mead's claim that the individual is unique and creative? Mead approaches this question from two directions: he posits spontaneity for the individual through what he terms the "I," and he speaks of how no two individuals can mirror a community or a society in an identical fashion, for each self reflects the whole "from its own particular and unique standpoint within that process . . . just as every monad in the Leibnizian universe mirrors that universe from a different point of view" (p. 201).

Given this view of the self as a reflection of the community, we might ask how an individual can criticize this community when he or she is but a reflection of it, when his or her character is so intimately bound up with it. Mead suggests that one can distance oneself from a particular social system by contemplating it from the

10. *MSS*, pp. 162–63. I should emphasize here that for Mead the generalized other exists in relation to various communities, and while it is possible to conceive of a community as a nation whose members share traditions, there are many types of groups or subgroups which have generalized others. "Some of them are concrete social classes or subgroups, such as political parties, clubs, corporations, which are all actually functional social units, in terms of which their individual members are directly related to one another. The others are abstract social classes or subgroups, such as the class of debtors and the class of creditors, in terms of which their individual members are related to one another only more or less indirectly" (p. 157).

perspective of a more encompassing social order. "The only way in which we can react against the disapproval of the entire community is by setting up a higher sort of community which in a certain sense out-votes the one we find" (pp. 167–68). Mead was a supporter of cosmopolitan organizations, such as the League of Nations, and viewed them as a means of bringing civilization to a point at which communication would be possible between peoples of diverse ethnic and cultural backgrounds. Through communication we would come to share the perspectives of others by taking the "role of the other" once thought to be totally alien to ourselves. From a wide-ranging sociological and historical perspective we can criticize the present through the eyes of the "universal."[11]

But how does an individual come to take a critical perspective on his or her own society if it is the source of his or her own self? In answering this question, we will see that Mead is committed to balancing the social with the creativity of the individual. The locus of change in society is the individual, for it is the individual who brings spontaneity to the social scene. In discussing the spontaneous, Mead distinguishes between the "I" and "me," the former being the seat of spontaneity, and both being interpreted as functional terms.

Mead refers to the self that is known, the only self we can grasp, as the "me," and to that which is aware of this social object, the presumed subject, as the "I" (p. 173). The "I" does not, and cannot, know itself; it is only aware of the object, the "me." In other words, for the "I" to become known, it must become an object, a "me," thereby losing its status as an "I." The "I" is known only in memory; having once been aware of a "me," it is transformed into a "me," an empirical self, an object of another "I."[12]

If you ask, then, where directly in your own experience the "I" comes in, the answer is that it comes in as a historical figure. It is what you were a second ago that is the "I" of the "me." It is another "me" that has to take

11. "We determine what the world has been by the anxious search for the means of making it better, and we are substituting the goal of a society aware of its own values and minded intelligently to pursue them, for the city not built with hands eternal in the heavens" (*PP*, p. 90).

12. George Herbert Mead, "The Mechanism of Social Consciousness," in *Selected Writings*, pp. 140–41. "The Social Self," in *Selected Writings*, pp. 142–43.

that rôle. You cannot get the immediate response of the "I" in the process. [*MSS*, p. 174]

Mead refers to the "I" as a presupposition which is not presented to consciousness except in the objective case.[13] The "I" appears as the initiator of the social act in which we are engaged, and we are often surprised by the action initiated by the "I." One never fully knows oneself because the "I," the seat of the unexpected, is beyond one's knowledge, because knowledge can only be knowledge of objects. "The 'I' is the response of the organism to the attitudes of the others; the 'me' is the organized set of attitudes of others which one himself assumes. The attitudes of the others constitute the organized 'me,' and then one reacts toward that as an 'I' " (*MSS*, p. 175).

This reaction or initiated action of the "I" introduces uncertainty and novelty into the individual's experience. I am never quite sure how my "I" will react to a given situation, even if I am somewhat familiar with the situation. The "I" is often directed toward the future, whereas the "me," as the social self, is a function of the past and the present.[14] Just how the "I" will respond to a given circumstance is not fully determined by that circumstance; in fact, the "I" can help to redefine the situation by the way in which it reacts to it. In reacting, it initiates novel responses or sets of responses in various ways, thereby altering the situation. "The 'I' gives the sense of freedom, of initiative. The situation is there for us to act in a self-conscious fashion. We are aware of ourselves, and of what the situation is, but exactly how we will act never gets into experience until after the action takes place" (*MSS*, pp. 177–78).

However, to say that the "I" gives rise to novel responses does not mean that its responses are absolutely novel, for if we are to interact with others, our responses must bear a relationship to the given social context. As a matter of fact, Mead's discussion (pp.

---

13. Mead, "The Social Self," p. 142; hereafter referred to as *SS*.

14. "Hence the 'me' is both the past and the social situation to which the 'I' responds, and its response may be an action which is more than an adjustment to the passive 'me,' since the 'I' is often motivated by the recognition of ends which lie in the future. Thus it is the 'me' that is conservative." Andrew J. Reck, "The Philosophy of George Herbert Mead (1863–1931)," *Tulane Studies in Philosophy* 12 (1963): 29–30.

175–78) suggests degrees of novelty and uncertainty in the individual's responses, which, of course, implies degrees of similarity and
certainty. Further, while it is true that, for Mead, the "me" exists
when one is conscious of it, it is also true that the "me" has a latent
existence by virtue of the presence of previously internalized behaviors. To be conscious of the "me," I must take the role of the other
or, if we are speaking of a more fully developed self, the generalized
other. Both entail repertoires of learned behaviors. I might also add
that the "I" avails itself of these repertoires in its responses.

But how are we to understand the introduction of novelty into
what has appeared up until this point to be a deterministic model?
After all, the social object, the "me," comes into being in relation
to the given social order, and one can criticize the present order
only by viewing it from an alternative, more inclusive, social order
(which may itself be determined). This more inclusive perspective
might only be new in regard to the breadth of its vision. Does this
vision actually include truly novel elements, or is it merely a different perspective on the given? Mead wants to argue that different
perspectives reveal the novel, that there is true novelty, and that
novelty can be discussed in terms of the I-pole of the person. (I use
the term *pole* to emphasize the contrasting characteristics of the "I"
and the "me," not to reify what Mead intends as functional distinctions. On the other hand, there is some question as to whether the
distinctions should be seen as solely functional, as we will see
shortly).

Mead uses two closely connected arguments to support his pos-
tulate of a non-determined element in a person's experience, each
of which deals with the relation of the past to the future, and hence
with the temporal nature of reality. First, he emphasizes that novelty and chance are aspects of the natural universe, and that, since
human beings are participants in this universe, their actions are
also subject to chance. The "me" that we anticipate is not the "me"
that we find on the other side of our actual response to situations,
because the situations in which we find ourselves are open—that
is, they allow for alternative courses of action.

We distinguish that individual who is doing something from the "me" who
puts the problem up to him. The response enters into his experience only
when it takes place. If he says he knows what he is going to do, even there

he may be mistaken. He starts out to do something and something happens to interfere. The resulting action is always a little different from anything which he could anticipate. [p. 177]

Of course, one could simply say that Mead is confusing epistemological concerns with metaphysics—that our not knowing what will happen does not mean that we are non-determined and free, but only that we appear to be free, due to ignorance. However, Mead argues for, and is convinced of, the actual existence of novelty. Chance and novelty are part of the fabric of the universe, so to speak. To understand the evolution of biological forms, for example, is to appreciate the importance of the novel, the mutation, in the scheme of things. For Mead, Parmenidean models of the universe—those that do not allow for becoming, for existence and nonexistence combining to yield unique events—are fundamentally misguided. "For a Parmenidean reality does not exist. Existence involves non-existence. . . . The world is a world of events" (PP, p. 1). He sees time itself as dependent upon the novel, because, if there were no (novel) events, the universe would be what it is not, a closed universe; and, as in any closed system, there would merely be movement, a shifting of elements without direction. Time entails direction, and for direction there must be the emergence of the novel event.[15]

On the other hand, according to Mead's second approach to the issue of determinism, freedom cannot simply be equated with chance or novelty. There is freedom because, as reflective, role-taking creatures, we are able to view various aspects of problems that arise. When different responses to a certain stimulus are possible, and when those possible responses conflict with one another, we have a problem. Human beings are unique in their capacity to both have and solve problems, and this capacity is intimately connected with their ability to view things from alternative perspectives, which in turn is related to their capacity for taking the roles

15. "It seems to me that the extreme mathematization of recent science in which the reality of motion is reduced to equations in which change disappears in an identity, and in which space and time disappear in a four dimensional continuum of indistinguishable events which is neither space nor time is a reflection of the treatment of time as passage without becoming" (PP, p. 19).

of others. In discussing Mead's views of perceptual conflicts, Miller makes the following statement, which can be applied to conflicts or problems in general from Mead's standpoint: "Under these circumstances, the individual is in a situation in which he may construct ideationally a new act or a newly proposed hypothesis or a new organization of events aimed at permitting the impeded act of adjustment to continue. Here we have the construction of a new perspective."[16]

The "I" reacts and initiates (new) acts; it "both calls out the 'me' and responds to it" (*MSS*, p. 178). If the (organized) "me" becomes disorganized—that is, experiences conflicting attitudes—the "I" which reacts has a problem. Its solution will be novel because what is, the "me," will have to be reorganized, and this reorganization, this new synthesis, cannot be predicted from the past "me." Conflict calls for resolution, and the resolution that emerges is related to, but not entirely determined by, that which gave rise to the conflict. The new comes into being because there are problems to be solved, while ends and goals are established by a self-conscious creature in response to the push and pull of experience.[17] The connection between this approach and Mead's other approach to the refutation of determinism is that whereas problems often arise because the universe actually contains novelty and chance, such problems call for solutions in the form of new behaviors.

It is important to note Mead's claims that the "I" and the "me" are functional distinctions. The "I" is not a (metaphysical) substance, neither is the "me." Maurice Natanson points out that "the distinction between the 'I' and the 'me' is, for Mead, a methodological one. In experience, in actual life situations, the self in its 'I' and 'me' aspects is an integral unity that may be called the 'personality.'

16. Miller, *George Herbert Mead*, p. 216. We might compare Mead here with Marx: "We pre-suppose labour in a form that stamps it as exclusively human. A spider conducts operations that resemble those of a weaver, and a bee puts to shame many an architect in the construction of her cells. But what distinguishes the worst architect from the best of bees is this, that the architect raises his structure in imagination before he erects it in reality. . . . [The labourer] realises a purpose of his own that gives the law to his modus operandi, and to which he must subordinate his will." Karl Marx, *Capital*, vol. 1, p. 178.

17. See ch. 4 below for further discussion and criticism of Mead's views on conflict.

The two phases of 'personality,' in this context, are stability and novelty."[18]

Even if Mead is not making metaphysical claims regarding the "I" and the "me," he must still face the issue of how his description of the self and its genesis can account for the unity of the personality. The reason for the difficulty here is that we have been told that the unity of the self is to be seen in terms of the generalized other, me-phase of personality. But how can the personality be maintained as a unity if it has an I-phase of unpredictable responses? In order to comprehend how Mead can regard the phases, or poles, of stability and novelty as aspects of a unitary personality, we must examine his views on systemic change. Mead understands change in terms of the emergence of one system from another, and the relation between continuity and discontinuity, between stability and novelty, must be viewed in this light. This, in turn, provides insight into how a personality can be said to have a pole of novelty and yet maintain unity.

Suppose we have a certain ecology of plant and animal life, one that is centered on a pond, say. The pond, together with its plant and animal life, constitutes a system in which the various elements play a variety of interdependent roles. If a new species or a new organism is introduced, because it evolves or emerges due to a mutation of a previously existing form, for example, the present ecosystem may undergo modification. Let us assume a modification occurs which takes the form of accommodating the new organism, so that the old system of interaction is altered to produce a new system that includes the new organism. The stage between the old and new systems is one of adjustment, in which the new biological form exists along with the system(s) in a state of limbo, being neither the past state of things nor the state to come. This phase of

18. Maurice Natanson, *The Social Dynamics of George Herbert Mead*, p. 17. This passage ends with the following quote from Mead: "The self is essentially a social process going on with these two distinguishable phases" (*MSS*, p. 178). The immediately preceding line in Mead's text reads: "Taken together they constitute a personality as it appears in social experience." Confusion might arise here because Mead often refers to the "I" *and* "me" as self, while in other contexts the self is first and foremost the "me"; for example, he says: "Recognizing that the self cannot appear in consciousness as an 'I,' that it is always an object, i.e., a 'me' . . ." (Mead, *SS*, p., 142). I follow the more restrictive usage of the term *self* and reserve the term *personality* for the combination of the "I" and the "me."

adjustment entails what Mead terms *sociality*. "The social character of the universe we find in the situation in which the novel event
is in both the old order and the new which its advent heralds. Sociality is the capacity of being several things at once" (*PP,* p. 49).
For Mead, the being in between entailed in sociality is found not
only in the world of (conscious) social animals; it is a way of addressing the relationships between a variety of systems.[19]

When the new form has established its citizenship the botanist can exhibit
the mutual adjustments that have taken place. The world has become a
different world because of the advent, but to identify sociality with this
result is to identify it with system merely. It is rather the stage betwixt and
between the old system and the new that I am referring to. If emergence is
a feature of reality this phase of adjustment, which comes between the
ordered universe before the emergent has arisen and that after it has come
to terms with the newcomer, must be a feature also of reality. [p. 47]

To further illustrate Mead's concept of sociality, we turn to his
views regarding the relation of past to present. For Mead, the past
does not exist as fixed, as if written on a scroll that can be unrolled
and read to find out what really happened. The past only becomes
what it is in relation to the present. It is not that the past is without
reality; it is that the past is altered by its relation to the present.
With the occurrence of a novel event, the past must be reinterpreted
in light of this event. But it is not only reinterpreted, if by "reinterpreted" we mean a merely subjective reading of what has taken
place. The past has actually become a different past because its locus of reality is the present.[20] On the one hand, the past and the

19. "Now what we are accustomed to call social is only a so-called consciousness
of such a process, but the process is not identical with the consciousness of it, for
that is an awareness of the situation. The social situation must be there if there is to
be consciousness of it" (*PP,* p. 48). This should not be interpreted, however, to make
consciousness irrelevant to situations; (self-) consciousness and (reflective) intelligence truly do make a difference for Mead.

20. If one were to ask Mead how different standpoints can be objectively valid,
he would point for clarification to the Einsteinian revolution in thought. "A consequence of the principle of relativity is that if any perspective is objectively real, that
is, not subjective or 'in the mind' of an individual, then at least two systems (reference systems) are involved. Just as a physical object can be said to be at rest or in
motion only in relation to some other body (or consentient set), so motion, rest,
acceleration, increase in mass of a body in motion, or, in general, qualities that were
traditionally thought to be *properties* of bodies are real only because of *relations*
between and among bodies" (Miller, *George Herbert Mead,* p. 199).

future have no existence because there is only the present; on the other, they are that out of which the present comes into being and into which it passes, because the present is not an eternal present. The past, then, is unchanging in that it is what has happened, and yet changes in that what has happened has the only existence possible for it in the present, a present that has come to be through the upsurge of the novel, the emergent.

It is idle, at least for the purposes of experience, to have recourse to a "real" past within which we are making constant discoveries; for the past must be set over against a present within which the emergent appears, and the past, which must then be looked at from the standpoint of the emergent, becomes a different past. The emergent when it appears is always found to follow from the past, but before it appears it does not, by definition, follow from the past. [*PP*, p. 2]

The relationship of an old system to a new system entails the relationship of past to present, though the present is often not the new system in its full glory, but the betwixt-and-between of sociality.[21] In such circumstances the system(s) with the emergent—to employ a variant of Sartre's terminology—is what it is not and is not what it is. I should again note that sociality, as the being in between systems, is not limited to biological evolution. As such, however, it relates directly to the question of how the "I" and the "me" are to be understood as aspects of a unified personality which is in the process of becoming.

During the process of adjustment that takes place by reflective intelligence, the individual must occupy two systems at once—the old system, the world that was there and taken for granted, the generalized other or the Me, and that new order constructed by virtue of the activity of the creative

21. It is worth noting that for all Mead's apparent indebtedness to Hegel on the question of the relation of past to present, when it comes to the importance of novelty and the independence of systems, he parts company with Hegel. Mead reflects Hegel's influence in seeing the relational nature of past and present (the present "absorbing" the past into itself, and thereby altering the past by its relation to it), but there is no present for Mead, in the sense of an eternal present, that overreaches the actual diversity of systems. For Hegel, there is indeed contingency in the universe, but it is due to the impotence of nature in failing to fully actualize the Idea. See my paper "Engels, Darwin, and Hegel's Idea of Contingency," *Studies in Soviet Thought* 21 (1980): 211–19.

I, an order which will lead to adjustment and enable the individual to continue in a new system.[22]

The change in the "me," which was "constituted" by a generalized other, to a new "me," entails sociality because it is a change from an old me-system to a new one. Systemic changes occur continually in the natural world, but only in the human world are they accompanied by reflective intelligence. The capacity to take the role of the other leads to the internalization of the other, thereby giving rise to a self which is multi-perspectival. The various perspectives are aspects of an integrated object known as the self or me-system, which mirrors the generalized other, while the element of novelty, the I-pole, transforms the personality by modifying this object-self. (To be more exact, one should speak not only of a system of society being embodied as a whole in *the* generalized other, but of numerous [sub]systems, generalized others, which constitute the whole of society. See note 10.)

But the animal could never reach the goal of becoming an object to itself as a whole until it could enter into a larger system within which it could play various rôles. . . . It is this development that a society whose life process is mediated by communication has made possible. It is here that mental life arises—with this continual passing from one system to another, with the occupation of both in passage and with the systematic structures that each involves. It is the realm of continual emergence. [*PP*, p. 85]

Mead often speaks of how one is not able to be a buyer without also being able to take the role of seller, for unless one can take the role of the other, one cannot play one's own role. As we take these roles, we become sensitized to being self and other and to living in between. To take a simple example, I am speaking with my boss about business, when he or she suddenly invites me to dinner with his or her family, a dinner for friends, so that I find myself between the business relationship (role) and a relationship (role) of friendship. It is only because I can take different roles—employee, boss, friend—and internalize various generalized others, that I have a self; a self is a system of behaviors that one is aware of through the internalized other.

22. Miller, *George Herbert Mead,* pp. 203–04.

However, since the I-pole is capable of responding in a novel fashion to the "me" that has been, personality (the combination of the "I" and the "me") does not merely play at previously learned roles but can undergo alteration. An old self is then related to a new self, as the past is to the present, a present that is coming to, or has come to, include this past. The state between old and new requires living in sociality—being and not being oneself as one becomes other than what one was in the transition to what one will be. Of course, this implies some relationship between the so-called old and new selves; yet, it is a relationship that cannot be known in advance, for the novel, the emergent, makes of the past what it will, and only then can the relationship between them be known. The me-systems are related, but the old system does not overreach and include the new system, so to speak, while the new system does overreach the past and include it within itself.

The I-pole or phase, as the initiator of action as well as what reacts to the "me," can never be an object of consciousness as it acts. Thus, while Mead's concept of sociality is of assistance in characterizing how the unity of the personality is to be understood as a non-static continuity, it fails to explain the sense we have of being conscious initiators of actions, novel or otherwise, of being conscious of "I" as well as of "me." According to Mead, we are conscious of the "I as self" only after the "I" has performed its (novel) deed and has in turn been converted to the "me" as object. Mead does say, though, that we often *feel* as if there is a "running current of awareness of what we do which is distinguishable from the consciousness of the field of stimulation."[23] Thus I see myself acting and am conscious of myself as actor, subject, so that the "I" is accessible without being converted into a "me" as object. Mead's position cannot allow for such a formulation, however. The "I" must become a "me" if it is to be known, but if it is an object of consciousness, it is no longer an "I." How, then, does Mead account for the feeling we have of being both observer and observed at the same time?

He argues that the so-called observer consciousness, the subject, the seeming "I," is "not the actual 'I' who is responsible for the conduct in *propria persona*—he is rather the response which one

<hr/>

23. Mead, *SS*, p. 144.

makes to his own conduct" (*SS*, p. 145). The so-called observer "I" comes in not as the initiator "I" but as an "I" that has become a "me" after responding to what was done or said in the original act. "The action with reference to the others calls out responses in the individual himself—there is then another 'me' criticising, approving, and suggesting, and consciously planning, i.e., the reflective self" (p. 145). The "me" that comes into being after the action of the "I" is actually the source of the feeling of the "running current of awareness," and it can give rise to this feeling because of the immediacy with which one can respond both to others and to oneself. Stimulus calls out response. For example, I speak to the other, and as I speak, I immediately hear myself speaking. I speak and hear at virtually the same instant, which means that I can respond or react to what I say almost as I say it. Mead tells us that "if one pronounces and hears himself pronounce the word 'table,' he has aroused in himself the organized attitudes of his response to that object, in the same fashion as that in which he has aroused it in another."[24] I am only conscious of these attitudes, however, in so far as they are brought to (self-) consciousness as aspects of the "me." I say to you, "Boy, do I love chocolate," and in effect hear the response, "But it's so bad for you." I experience these statements as if the same "I" said them and understood them, as if there were no distinction between the "I" and the "me." In reality the response has not only drawn on prior experience, it has been brought to my awareness in an objectified form. The running commentary that I am often conscious of, and that I associate with myself as subject, is due to the reflexive echo from the "me." The "I" that is aware of this commenting "me" is not the "I" that initiated the response, for that "I" is now objectified as this "me." It is a new "I" that is aware of the "me" as the stream of consciousness has moved on. Mead claims, on the other hand, that there are times when I am so immersed in what I am doing, so involved in the "world that is there," that I do not comment on, reflect on, myself and my actions, and the "me" disappears. "Where we are intensely preoccupied with the objective world, this accompanying awareness disappears. We have to recall the experience to become aware that we have been involved as selves, to produce the self-

24. Mead, "The Genesis of the Self and Social Control," p. 287.

consciousness which is a constituent part of a large part of our experience" (*SS*, p. 145).

The fact that one can act without a self-conscious self is in itself not a remarkable claim, especially in a century given to a rather obsessive preoccupation with the unconscious. Yet, Mead's model suggests more than this, the absence of the self due to lack of self-consciousness. The self as an actuality disappears unless one is actively reflecting on it. Further, when new actions or moral principles are called for, the new actions or principles are first "chosen" and then integrated into the (new) self, so that the (new) self does not consciously choose its values, but has them chosen for it. In discussing the creation and acceptance of new values, Mead declares that "the new self that answers to this new situation can appear in consciousness only after this new situation has been realized and accepted. The new self can not enter into the field as the determining factor because he is consciously present only after the new end has been formulated and accepted" (p. 148).

This is only another way of saying that the self as an object found in memory, albeit at times an almost immediate memory, cannot institute new values, but has them instituted for it. The fact that the initiator "I" is known only as converted into an object "me," has led Maurice Natanson to make the following remark:

It is only the other who sees the individual *in his acts*. In a restricted yet important sense, then, the other knows more about the individual than the individual himself does, for he observes the "I" in the acts that reveal the self [the personality], whereas the individual requires an act of reflection to view those acts.[25]

Though Natanson qualifies his use of the word *know*, it would have been more accurate not to use it at all in this passage. Because the other sees me act does not mean that he or she knows me better than I know myself, for he or she must also reflect on my responses to be self-consciously aware of them, to know them. But Natanson's comments do point to another important aspect of the issue under consideration: one can never be a self unless one is an object of knowledge, so that whatever knowledge one has of one's own

25. Natanson, *Social Dynamics of Mead*, p. 60; original emphasis.

creative and spontaneous side(s) can only be had when removed from the spontaneous by being converted into an object. The creative activities of the "I" are real for Mead, but they can only be known in retrospect. In other words, we are free, that is, not determined, but our freedom has a source outside the self, is something that happens to the self and is made to happen by a subject out of reach. This, in turn, leaves one wondering whether the notion of reflective, purposeful behavior has any meaning if the "I" that acts is itself never the "I" that can self-consciously demand of itself a certain pattern of behavior. We strive for ends, according to Mead, but the ends are initiated by and/or responded to by an "I" that one cannot directly tap and whose spontaneity happens to the "me," which comes to exhibit its creativity. Of course, in Mead's view we do possess a reflective intelligence, but just how it affects the "I" is open to question.

There is indeed ambiguity in Mead's view of the "I." In places he treats it merely as a necessary fiction, a needed presupposition for the "me," since for every object there must be a subject. But Mead's claim to be dealing with the I–me distinction solely in functional terms appears to break down once the "I" becomes the seat of the spontaneous and creative in the universe, a "home" that can rescue us from determinism. For, if it is to rescue us from a deterministic universe, then the novelty it introduces must be seen not only in functional terms, but as altering the fabric of the universe. Pfuetze has suggested in his book on Mead and Buber, that there is a tension between Mead the empirical scientist who must emphasize the me-pole, the empirically intelligible self, and Mead the metaphysician for whom the "I," as the sphere of novelty and creativity, lies beyond the confines of scientific method.[26] Mead makes moral and metaphysical claims regarding the place of novelty in the universe, and the I-pole must carry the weight of these assertions. On the other hand, novelty for Mead is not merely a metaphysical assumption, because it is itself an empirical truth, an observable phenomenon. For example, nature gives rise to the novel, the mutation that can be observed and whose existence and repercussions must be acknowledged as part of the fabric of the universe. In Mead's

26. Paul E. Pfuetze, *The Social Self,* pp. 95–96.

scheme, the human being appears as the organism whose nature includes novelty, though the subject—the "I," the seat of spontaneity and novelty—remains a thing-in-itself, a noumenal phantom.

In the last few paragraphs, I have raised several issues that are of interest to Sartre, especially the question of the relation of the spontaneous to the object-self, the "me." These issues serve as a transition to our consideration of Sartre, who has been viewed as the redeemer of the spontaneous and the scourge of those who wish to reduce the sense of self to a mere object of cognition.

CHAPTER TWO

Sartre

Consciousness, Self, and the Other

IT IS WITH SOME TREPIDATION THAT I ADD YET ANOTHER CHAPTER to the vast literature on Sartre which is already available. My goal, however, is a modest one. I plan to discuss Sartre's views on consciousness, reflection, and the self in the early works in order to augment Mead's conception of reflection and selfhood. This is not to say that I necessarily agree with Sartre's position on these matters, but that certain elements of his thought highlight the strengths and weaknesses of Mead's position, while Mead does the same for Sartre. This chapter is expository; a comparison and critique of Mead and Sartre follows. In Part Two I will cast aside those elements in Mead and Sartre that are inadequate for the task of understanding self-determination, while retaining several key insights.

It is no secret that many professional philosophers look upon Sartre first and foremost as a novelist, playwright, and psychologist (of sorts), whose so-called philosophical works avail themselves of literary devices and psychological insights. It is worth noting in this regard that while Sartre saw his earliest philosophical endeavors as working to enhance his literary skill, he came to deny psychology a base outside philosophy. Regarding his youthful approach to philosophy, Sartre stated in an interview held in 1975: "I decided that I would study philosophy, considering it at that point to be simply a methodical description of man's inner states, of his psychological life, all of which would serve as a method and instrument for my literary works."[1] He goes on to say: "I was surprised a moment

---

1. Sartre, "The Interview," p. 6.

ago to learn that some of the contributors speak of my psychology. There is philosophy, but there is no psychology. Psychology does not exist; either it is idle talk or it is an effort to establish what man is, starting from philosophical notions."[2]

With Sartre, as with Mead, psychological and philosophical themes are often interwoven. It is appropriate, then, that we begin this chapter with one of Sartre's characterizations of roles in order to see how he transforms this social-psychological construct—akin to Mead's concept of role-taking—into a unique vision of consciousness and selfhood.

The notion of role-taking is crucial to Mead's concept of the self, whereas for Sartre the nature of consciousness modifies and limits the extent to which one can *be* the role one takes. In *Being and Nothingness* Sartre gives an account of the role of waiter, an account that has become rather well known. As we observe a waiter performing his or her assigned role in a café, we note that the waiter's actions do not seem quite right. "His movement is quick and forward, a little too precise, a little too rapid. He comes toward the patrons with a step a little too quick. . . . All his behavior seems to us a game."[3] And we are told that what the waiter is really doing "is playing *at being* a waiter in a café" (original emphasis). For Sartre, one plays at a role in order to become the role, while in actuality no one is fully the role that he or she plays or seeks to assume. The "public" demands that one act in a certain fashion, play a role in a certain way, but a person is not reducible to a role. A person possesses consciousness, and hence is referred to by Sartre as a *for-itself:* that which can be for itself, conscious of itself. On the other hand, a thing is but an *in-itself* for Sartre; it is incapable of having an awareness of itself because it is incapable of distancing itself from itself, of somehow being other than itself. The waiter in the café can never be just a waiter, no matter how hard he or she plays at the role of waiter, because he or she can be conscious of being a waiter. "But if I represent myself as him, I am not he [the waiter]; I am separated from him as the object from the subject, separated *by nothing,* but this nothing isolates me from him. I can

2. Ibid., p. 8.
3. Sartre, *Being and Nothingness*, p. 59; hereafter referred to as *BN*.

not be he, I can only play *at being* him. . . . I am a waiter in the mode of *being what I am not*" (*BN,* p. 60; original emphasis).

I am and am not the waiter, because I am aware of being or playing (at the role of) waiter, and my awareness separates me from the role. I am separated from it (as if) by nothing, consciousness being this nothing. Consciousness is all important for Sartre, even if he describes it as "nothing." But what is Sartre driving at by referring to consciousness in this manner?

One way to approach this is to understand that what Sartre is trying to say is that consciousness is aware of objects while also "knowing" that it is *not* the objects of which it is aware.[4] It is transparent, lucid, and always aware of itself in being aware, but it is nothing in particular. Sartre also makes the claim that consciousness is *ekstatic:* it stands outside of itself; it is always beyond itself; it is never identical to itself. And as such, it is thoroughly temporal. So, we must understand consciousness as temporal, while at the same time it is "nothing." Hegel may be of some assistance here, for his linkage of time and negativity in the *Philosophy of Nature* provides one way of understanding how temporality and consciousness (as nothing) are linked for Sartre.

Hegel describes time in this work as *pure* negativity. By this he means that it is a negativity that is always negating, and that what it negates is itself. If we think of clock time, it is readily apparent that that which is, the present, cannot sustain itself, that it immediately becomes the past. The present is the negation of itself. "Time, as the negative unity of self-externality . . . is that being which, inasmuch as it *is,* is *not,* and inasmuch as it is *not, is.*"[5]

Time as pure externality is always distant from itself, external to itself, at the juncture described above, and it is this externality only because it is imbued with, or is, negativity. This negativity entails a continuous negating of itself, without the negation leading (as yet) to the dialectical synthesis of the negation of the negation (with which Hegel is usually associated). In other words, in the above

4. I am using the term *object* here simply to differentiate between that which appears and the consciousness, or subject, to which it appears.

5. G. W. F. Hegel, *The Philosophy of Nature,* p. 34, para. 258; original emphasis. See my book *The Self-Winding Circle: A Study of Hegel's System,* pp. 42–54.

conception of time as self-negating, the dialectical second negation, the one that would synthesize the negatives into an affirmative, never takes place. Time is always going outside itself, separating from itself, as the present is negated in the flow of time.

For Sartre, consciousness is the nothing that separates from itself in the act of becoming aware. One cannot be aware of something without at the same time being apart from it, for "consciousness of anything has to be supported by a negative ¬elation—without which the difference between consciousness and its object would collapse."[6] But note that consciousness is not only in a negative relation to some object outside itself, it is also in a negative relation to itself, just as time is. It cannot be aware of itself without becoming negative, because it is this negative relation that allows consciousness to be aware—to be aware of objects and to be aware of itself in being aware of objects.

Consciousness is ekstatic. This means not only that it is dispersed through time, but that it finds itself aware because it separates from itself and is thus thoroughly temporal. The nothing, consciousness, that allows the object to appear while not being it, is precisely the same nothing that becomes temporality in the activity of what Sartre calls *nihilation,* that is, negation.

The For-itself—if we stick to the primary ekstases . . . can and must at the same time fulfill these three requirements: (1) to not-be what it is, (2) to be what it is not, (3) to be what it is not and not-be what it is—within the unity of a perpetual referring. Here we are dealing with three ekstatic dimensions; the meaning of the ekstasis is distance from self. It is impossible to conceive of a consciousness which would not exist in these three dimensions. [*BN,* p. 137]

As Present, Past and Future—all at the same time—the For-itself dispersing its being in three dimensions is temporal due to the very fact that it nihilates itself. [*BN,* p. 142]

Sartre views consciousness as able to be aware of itself because it is not identical with itself due to its nihilation of itself. Without developing Hegel's dialectic of time any further, we can at least say

6. Herbert L. Dreyfus and Piotr Hoffman, "Sartre's Changed Conception of Consciousness: From Lucidity to Opacity," p. 239.

that time cannot maintain itself solely as pure externality, for as such there would be no continuity to which to relate its individual moments. One would have only discontinuous "nows," not the flow of time, if there were no underlying unity or continuity. For time to be time there must obviously be continuity as well as discontinuity. And this is the same conclusion that Sartre must, and does, draw regarding consciousness. While consciousness is always distant from itself, this distance implies a relationship to itself, so that consciousness must in some way be unified, as well as dispersed, in its nihilation, or negation, of itself. Consciousness, in Sartre's terms, is a detotalized totality—a discontinuity that is also continuous. In sum, for consciousness, as well as for time, there must be unity if there is to be difference, distance from "self." I will return to the question and nature of the unity of consciousness for Sartre in chapter 3.

However, one must not overplay the unity of consciousness in Sartre's thinking. It is, after all, the nature of consciousness to be ahead of itself, to be spontaneous, to be without foundation, to be nothing. The lack of a substantial, or substance-like, foundation yields a radically free consciousness and leads to the psychological need to overcome this terrifying freedom by transforming consciousness into a thing, an in-itself. According to Sartre, consciousness tries to prevent and arrest its spontaneity, so to speak, and in so doing gives rise to reflection. "By reflection the for-itself, which has lost itself outside itself, attempts to put itself inside its own being" (BN, p. 153). Up until this point we have been discussing consciousness in general, but in Sartre there is a crucial distinction between pre-reflective and reflective consciousness. Further, there are two varieties of reflection: impure and pure reflection. Before proceeding to address the intricacies of his account of reflection, I would like to clarify the relation between pre-reflective and reflective consciousness in very general terms.

For Sartre, consciousness is first and foremost pre-reflective; it is aware of objects and experiences itself as aware of these objects, but it does not experience itself as an object.[7] A waiter can be aware

---

7. In discussing consciousness in general I have used the term *object* to denote what appears, but in speaking of reflection the term often carries with it the connotation of reification, as will be seen in what follows regarding impure reflection.

of performing the duties of a waiter without reflecting on or making herself or himself an object (of study)—that is, without reflecting on or thinking about his or her identity as a waiter. As such, he or she has a pre-reflective consciousness of being a waiter, although he or she is also in a certain sense distant from being a waiter, because consciousness is not that of which it is aware.

As I go about my daily routines in the world, I am aware that it is me, my consciousness, that engages in various acitivities and is aware of objects. During these activities I have an indirect, or pre-reflective, awareness of "self" without reflecting on myself as an object. Pre-reflective consciousness is never identical with itself, because it is in actuality the nihilation of itself; indeed, were it not for this nihilation, it would become a thing, an in-itself. Yet, Sartre tells us, pre-reflective consciousness wishes to have a stable identity, to be an in-itself, while remaining conscious, while remaining free. It longs to transform itself into a fixed object. To accomplish this impossible goal, consciousness turns on itself, that is, it reflects on itself.

One might think of pre-reflective consciousness as a mirror that not only reflects objects but also has the capacity to experience itself as it reflects objects. Reflection takes this a step further. The original "consciousness and object" becomes the object of a "new" consciousness, so that reflection not only reflects the original pre-reflective consciousness but also experiences itself in the process. Reflection, though, must not give rise to a totally new object; it must not distance itself to such an extent that it would make the original consciousness totally other, for to do so would be to make it no longer part of the same "stream of consciousness." Yet, there is an otherness present here that is deeper than that of the otherness found in the original distancing phenomenon of pre-reflective consciousness. Not only is there nihilation, but a deepening of the nihilation, the nothingness, that exists at the pre-reflective level. To further complicate matters, reflection can either be pure or impure, and thus far I have been using language more suited to impure reflection.

What Sartre terms "impure reflection" is a form of reflection that is primarily cognitive, giving rise to psychic objects; for example, one can and does make pre-reflective consciousness into an object (of study). Pure reflection, on the other hand, appears to be an apprehension in which the otherness of the pre-reflective remains closely connected to the reflective consciousness, so that the pre-reflective is not posited as an object, as it would be in impure reflection. For Mead, reflection is synonymous with self-consciousness and requires making or positing the self as an object, as in impure reflection. For Sartre, on the other hand, while reflection often entails making oneself into an object, it can also be seen as a deepening of the awareness of pre-reflective consciousness: one becomes hyper-aware of consciousness reflecting "reality" and itself without directly making the self into an object. "Pure reflection, the simple presence of the reflective for-itself to the for-itself reflected-on, is at once the original form of reflection and its ideal form . . . and it is that which must be won by a sort of katharsis" (BN, p. 155).

Pure reflection is the experience in which consciousness has insight into its ontological nature as a dispersed being, as a temporal being, without "deepening" that dispersal so as to give rise to impure reflection.[8] Impure reflection occurs much more frequently than pure reflection, according to Sartre, and it is to impure reflection that we must turn in order to understand what is usually thought of as self-consciousness and self-knowledge. However, before discussing impure reflection, I wish to raise the issue of the birth of consciousness, the for-itself—that is, the question of how the for-itself arises.

The question of the genesis of consciousness and self-consciousness, so crucial for Mead, is seen by Sartre as a metaphysical question, a "why" question, that is outside of the ontological concerns of Sartre's phenomenological approach. Yet, he cannot avoid the question of the birth, or coming to be, of consciousness, for the fact of birth seems to suggest the existence of a for-itself *without* a past, and this would violate Sartre's conception of the thoroughly temporal nature of consciousness. Sartre provides the following answer to the question of birth:

8. "The question was posed as to how authenticity is possible. It is possible only because the reflective consciousness, whose ordinary state is one of *impure* reflection, can purify itself. Because it can purify itself, consciousness apprehends its true ontological structure; it sees itself as an incomplete unity in dispersion, with no completed self-identity" (Phyllis Berdt Kenevan, 'Self-consciousness and the Ego in the Philosophy of Sartre," pp. 202–03; original emphasis.)

We do not have to ask why there can be a birth of consciousness, for consciousness can appear to itself only as a nihilation of in-itself—*i.e., as being already born.* . . . But one should not next raise *metaphysical* questions concerning the In-itself from which the For-itself was born. . . . All these questions fail to take into account the fact that it is through the For-itself that the Past in general can exist. [*BN,* p. 139; original emphasis]

The shock of the idea of an original appearance of consciousness, according to Sartre, is mollified when we realize that without the for-itself there is no past. One cannot answer the question of what the past would have been like before consciousness, because only the for-itself allows the past to exist as past. Once Sartre has dismissed the issue of origins in this manner, he proceeds to provide the psychological explanation outlined above for why and how the for-itself gives rise to (impure) reflection. He supposes that the for-itself desires to ground itself—due to its experience of the radical contingency and spontaneity of consciousness—by becoming its own object, by becoming an in-itself (while remaining a for-itself).

It is not simply that the problem of the birth of consciousness remains insoluble for Sartre, however; rather, it is a necessary axiom of his approach that one cannot explain the birth of consciousness. If one could solve the question of why (and how) my or any consciousness comes into being from a particular fetus or infant, the radical contingency that Sartre insists permeates the universe would not be quite so radical. If one could explain how consciousness emerges from the in-itself, there would be a source for the nothing, for consciousness; one would not have to regard it as an upsurge of nothing in being, to take Sartre's description. Something would give rise to nothing, which, in turn, would suggest that nothing, consciousness, is not the pure spontaneity Sartre claims it is. We have a peculiar reversal here of the maxim that something cannot come from nothing: for Sartre, nothing cannot come from something. Indeed, freedom appears to hinge on there being this nothing which, as the source of nihilation and spontaneity, is itself without a source of genesis. Sartre's radical dualism—the division of the world into the realm of consciousness, the for-itself, and the realm of things, the in-itself—makes it impossible for him to explain the emergence of consciousness from anything but an already developed consciousness. Mead's problem of the genesis of mind must remain a non-problem.

Impure reflection, on the other hand, appears to have something of a genesis, a genesis that is set in motion by the psychological need to arrest the spontaneity of consciousness. Impure reflection and the emergence of the ego, or self, go hand in hand. The ego is an object of consciousness that is produced as consciousness attempts to thwart its spontaneity through reflection. This ego, properly speaking, should be called a quasi-object, because it is an object that has an especially intimate relationship with the consciousness whose object it is. For Sartre, there is no ego, or self, "behind" consciousness; the ego, or self, is constituted by consciousness. The conviction that the ego, or what can also be termed the self, is the result of the deepening operation of (impure) reflection is one of Sartre's most firmly held beliefs. He asserted this position in *The Transcendence of the Ego* and again forty years later in an interview.[9]

I wrote an article called "La Transcendance de l'ego," in which I held that the ego was a sort of quasi-object of consciousness and, consequently, was excluded from consciousness. I maintained that point of view even in *L'Etre et le Néant* [BN]; I would still maintain it today; but at this stage it is no longer a subject of my reflections. ["The Interview," p. 10]

Sartre then proceeds to argue regarding why the ego can not be "within" or "behind" consciousness, and in much the same terms as he had in *Being and Nothingness*—to place the ego within or behind consciousness would destroy the lucidity and freedom of consciousness, because the ego would then constitute and/or direct consciousness. However, Sartre does not want to say that the ego is just like any other thing or object of consciousness, for we do have a more intimate relationship with this object than we do with other objects. We often interpret ourselves and the world in the light of the ego, or psyche, we call our own, and it provides a context for our actions.[10]

9. Sartre, *The Transcendence of the Ego*, pp. 58–61; henceforth referred to as *TE*.

10. Joseph S. Catalano, *A Commentary on Jean-Paul Sartre's "Being and Nothingness,"* p. 131.

In reflecting on the pre-reflective, I distance myself from this (pre-reflective) consciousness so as to make a quasi-object of it. I give myself a quasi "outside," a "nature," and this outside is the self of so-called (scientific) psychological investigations. But this outside I give myself in reflection, this object of cognition, this self that I can observe and study, is not the most complete experience available to me of having an outside, of being an object. It is only in my relationships with other human beings that I fully experience what it is to be an object. "The for-itself sees itself almost as bestowing an outside on its own eyes, but this outside is purely virtual. We shall see later how being-for-others *realizes* the suggestion of this outside" (*BN*, p. 170; original emphasis). Sartre's account of a person's relationships with others is of crucial importance for the comparison with Mead in the next chapter, but first we must look more closely at the relationship between the self or ego, and consciousness.

If the self, or ego, arises only for a reflective consciousness, can we then say that pre-reflective consciousness is impersonal? According to Sartre's account in *The Transcendence of the Ego,* this appears to be the case; consciousness is always aware of itself but not always of having a self or ego.

We may therefore formulate our thesis: transcendental consciousness is an impersonal spontaneity. It determines its existence at each instant, without our being able to conceive anything *before* it. Thus each instant of our conscious life reveals to us a creation *ex nihilo*. Not a new *arrangement*, but a new existence. [*TE*, pp. 98–99, original emphasis]

In *Being and Nothingness,* Sartre reconsiders the issue. Consciousness is still regarded as a spontaneity, but he now argues that it is *indirectly* aware of "self" on the pre-reflective level; thus, there is a non-positional consciousness of "self" for every positional consciousness (of objects). Consciousness, we are told, is always a self-consciousness, though the "self" of which we are aware is not always the equivalent of the ego in this new account. While it can still be the quasi-object of consciousness known as the ego, it can also be the "selfness" of consciousness, the sense consciousness has of being a subject, a "self," that does not make itself into an object. In other words, Sartre introduces a new form of (indirect) self-awareness on the pre-reflective level, one that he did not advance in *The Transcendence of the Ego*. In *Being and Nothingness*, Sartre says:

Yet we need not conclude that the for-itself is a pure and simple "impersonal" contemplation. But the Ego is far from being the personalizing pole of a consciousness which without it would remain in the impersonal stage; on the contrary, it is consciousness in its fundamental selfness which under certain conditions allows the appearance of the Ego as the transcendent phenomenon of that selfness. [*BN*, p. 103]

Sartre argues that there is personal existence, which is not due to an ego but is rooted in the experience of *presence* that pre-reflective consciousness has by virtue of the fact that it is a diasporic unity (p. 103). Consciousness, in not being identical with itself, is aware of itself, is present to itself. Consciousness is beyond itself and remains aware of itself in its flight to the future; here the "self" is found as an ideal, as the limit of the flight of pre-reflective awareness.[11] But, in addition to a personal existence due to the limit of the awareness of pre-reflective consciousness, there is also *selfness*. It arises as consciousness deepens the negativity found in presence, thus becoming an "absent presence," and refers to itself in terms of what it is not, in terms of its possibilities (*BN*, pp. 103–4). "This free necessity of being—down there—what one is in the form of lack constitutes selfness or the second aspect of the person. In fact how can the person be defined if not as a free relation to himself?" (*BN*, p. 104).

This selfness, which I also refer to by the less ungainly phrase *sense of self*, is decidedly non-cognitive, for cognition is found only at the level of impure reflection, and the sense of self occurs at the pre-reflective level (and, perhaps, in a more perfected form on the level of pure reflection). As I move through the world, as I make my daily rounds in the world, a sense of self—of my possibilities, of that which I lack—permeates my pre-reflective consciousness. It is only because there is a plentitude of Being that there can be possibilities, but at the same time, for Sartre, it is only in relation to my possibilities that there is (my) world at all, properly speaking. I am always with myself, even when the self is not actively being produced by reflective consciousness in the form of an object. Sartre's posi-

11. Ibid., p. 109.

tion on the non-cognitive awareness of "self," through the sense of
self, seemingly allows him to avoid having to posit a self that
knows and another self that is known.[12] For cognitive knowledge
of the self, an object-self needs a subject-self to know it, and this
subject-self, in turn, needs another subject-self to know it as an
object, and so on. Mead, Sartre would claim, has this problem with
his I—me distinction; the subject self, the "I," remains merely an
observer, an observer that in itself can never be known, for to be
known is to become an object, as we have already seen.

The experience of selfness lies not in unceasing and unsatisfied
(impure) reflection, but in the sense of self found at the level of pre-
reflective consciousness. Existence precedes essence, as Sartre is
wont to say, and reflection entails a removal from existence, from
the world, through the creation of reified objects, essences, psychic
structures, which are then thought to be more real than the spontaneous consciousness that gave birth to them. To achieve cognitive
self-knowledge would require, for Sartre, a subject that could simultaneously be its own object. But he rejects the possibility of
simultaneity, for it could arise only by presupposing an ego "behind" consciousness making itself its own object. But the ego is not
behind experience observing it, it is "out there," so to speak, an
object of reflective consciousness similar to other objects. As such,
it is not identical with the awareness that gives rise to it, for consciousness separates itself from its objects; it is the nihilation of its
objects. Consciousness is aware that it *is not* the object of which it
is aware, and, hence, the object called the self, as a product of reflective consciousness, must be at a distance from the consciousness
that is supposed to be immediately aware of it. However, due to
"The Look" of the other, one can have what is in a certain sense
an immediate experience of being an object, and this takes place,
not on the level of reflective consciousness, but on the pre-reflective
level.

Sartre, as we have seen, argues that the self, or ego, is a quasi-
object of reflective consciousness. On the pre-reflective level I do
not have an "outside,"—that is, I am not an object (quasi or otherwise) for myself. Yet, it is on the pre-reflective level that I most

12. Kenevan, "Self-consciousness and the Ego in the Philosophy of Sartre,"
p. 197.

fully experience having an outside, a nature, an objective existence. If I am alone on the pre-reflective level and then find myself caught by the gaze of the other—as in Sartre's example of the Peeping Tom, who, while staring through a keyhole, suddenly finds himself looked at by an other—I am no longer the one who organizes the things of the world as my possibilities (*BN*, pp. 259–60). I have become but an object for the other. When dealing with the pre-reflective for-itself in isolation, in the absence of an other, it appears that there is no (object-) self, only an ideal self and a sense of self.[13] Now consciousness finds itself tossed into the world of objects through the look of the other, and as such has a self on the pre-reflective level.

The self comes to haunt the unreflective consciousness. Now the unreflective consciousness is a consciousness *of* the world. Therefore for the unreflective consciousness the self exists on the level of objects in the world; this role which devolved only on the reflective consciousness—the making-present of the self—belongs now to the unreflective consciousness. Only the reflective consciousness has the self directly for an [quasi] object. The unreflective consciousness does not apprehend the *person* directly or as *its* object; the person is presented to consciousness *in so far as the person is an object for the Other*. [*BN*, p. 260; original emphasis]

If one is to be seen as an object, there must be a subject doing the seeing. Without the other I cannot experience my objectiveness on the pre-reflective level, for as a pre-reflective consciousness I am my consciousness, I am my subjectivity, and I am indirectly aware of myself in having a sense of self. With the arrival of the other (who, Sartre tells us, is always present as a fact of human existence, although we cannot deduce the other from the ontological structure of the for-itself), I have the experience of being an object, of having my spontaneity arrested, of losing my freedom by becoming an ob-

13. "Let us imagine that moved by jealousy, curiosity, or vice I have just glued my ear to the door and looked through a keyhole. I am alone and on the level of a non-thetic self-consciousness. This means first of all that there is no self to inhabit my consciousness, nothing therefore to which I can refer my acts in order to qualify them. They are in no way *known;* I *am my acts* and hence they carry in themselves their whole justification. I am a pure consciousness *of* things, and things, caught up in the circuit of my selfness, offer to me their potentialities as the proof of my non-thetic consciousness (of) my own possibilities" (*BN*, p. 259; original emphasis).

ject among other objects. Yet I am not simply an object in the manner of an in-itself. I can dislodge myself from the objecthood created by the other, but to do so I must look upon and convert the other into an object. Hence, there is a war of each against the other, each trying to maintain his subjectivity against the Medusa look of the other.

The war, however, is a rather complex affair. It is rather easy to distinguish consciousness from the in-itself, because the modes of being of the for-itself and the in-itself are so radically different. Consciousness, on the other hand, has the same mode of being as the other, for both are consciousness, and the opponents in the battle must find a way to distinguish themselves from each other while sharing the same mode of being. Sartre tells us that numerical grounds for opposition will not do: "We do not have *two* or *several* consciousnesses here; numbering supposes an external witness and is the pure and simple establishment of exteriority. There can be an *Other* for the For-itself only in a spontaneous and prenumerical negation" (*BN*, p. 284; original emphasis). The prenumerical negation that separates consciousness from the other must be reciprocal. "Not only do I make myself not-be this other being by denying that he is me, I make myself not-be a being who is making himself not-be me" (pp. 284–85). The separation from the other proceeds in the following manner: the other nihilates, or negates, my being as consciousness through its capacity as consciousness to *not be* what appears to consciousness. I become not-selfness for the other; I become an object; and, in turn, I must refuse to be this object, referred to by Sartre as the *me*, that the other has produced. I must refuse to be the object-me that I am for the other, if I am to be subject and not object. However, this object-me, this alienated me, is crucial for creating and maintaining separation from the other.

I can not *not-be* the Other unless I assume my being-as-object for the Other. The disappearance of the alienated Me would involve the disappearance of the Other through the collapse of Myself. . . . Thus this Me which has been alienated and refused is simultaneously my bond with the Other and the symbol of our absolute separation. [*BN*, p. 285]

The me-as-object, my being-for-others, is my "outside," my "nature." I recognize and accept it as my outside. I am a subject that can and must become an object for other(s), for if I did not have the me-as-object as an outside, I would have no way of differentiating from the other (pp. 286–87). However, I do not have to remain solely this me. Because of the freedom of (my) consciousness to not be what it is, I can escape from the me which I am for the other and myself. My consciousness is then not reduced to the me but negates it, distances itself from it. Yet, I must also accept the me-as-object, for it serves as a boundary, a limit, that separates and protects consciousness from the other. As my "outer self," it is a shield necessary for defense. "Now we can grasp the nature of my Self[-]as-object: it is the limit between two consciousnesses as it is produced by the limiting consciousness and assumed by the limited consciousness" (p. 286).

As the limited consciousness I have become an object for the other, but in assuming this limit—that is, the me-as-object—I can reaffirm the freedom of my consciousness as the nothing which is *not* this me-as-object. I turn on the other, who has achieved subjectivity by asserting and refusing my me, and I declare this me as *not* self(ness). I thereby assert my subjectivity in the face of the other. The other, defining itself solely in terms of not-being me, has a rather vacuous pre-reflective self that is then easily converted into an object by my look.

By this very wrenching away which puts the Other in possession of my limit, I am already putting the Other out of play. . . . [He] is now what it depends on me to not-be, and thereby his transcendence is no longer a transcendence which *transcends me* toward himself but a purely contemplated transcendence, simply a *given* circuit of selfness. [p. 287; original emphasis]

We have here a version of Hegel's master and slave dialectic in which the roles of master and slave are continually being exchanged. Either I must be limited, or I must overcome this limit, this me-as-object, by limiting the other.[14] The motivation for this seesaw movement, Sartre informs us, is on the affective level. I am

14. Anyone familiar with Hegel's master and slave dialectic cannot help but be struck by Sartre's indebtedness to Hegel; yet, interestingly, in an interview in 1975, in response to a question regarding when he read Hegel, he states that "I knew of him through seminars and lectures, but I didn't study him until much later, around 1945." And to the question of when he discovered the dialectic, he retorts: "Late. After *L'Etre et le Néant* [*BN*]" ("The Interview," p. 9). *BN* was originally published in 1943.

afraid of the other, in that the other robs me of my freedom, my possibilities, when viewing me as an object. I experience shame before the other, for shame is to have an outside, a nature, to be fixed, to be an object. Sartre speaks of shame as "the feeling of an *original fall* . . . I have 'fallen' into the world in the midst of things and . . . I need the mediation of the Other in order to be what I am" (*BN*, pp. 288–89; original emphasis). Sartre would agree with Mead that we are not fully human unless we have a being-for-others, a mediated being, but for Sartre this being is also the primordial source of shame.

The account of the look in *Being and Nothingness* is Sartre's early contribution to the task of freeing the world from the demon of solipsism. By experiencing the transformation of myself under the gaze of others, I am convinced that there must be others. However, if solipsism is to be defeated, then the existence of the other(s) cannot be merely probable, it must be experienced as certain. I say "experienced" because Sartre's "proof" rests on the affective level of the look, the power of the look to make the presence of the other felt, and not on cognitively knowing or proving that there are others. But suppose I feel as if I am being "looked-at," to use Sartre's term, when there are no others empirically present to gaze at me. Wouldn't this weaken my conviction that there must be others? I feel ashamed, yet I look around and find there is no one before whom I should feel ashamed. I have been mistaken regarding the empirical presence of the other. Given this, "does not our certainty of the Other's existence take on a purely hypothetical character" (p. 275)?

In response, Sartre argues that the other is always in a sense present, a presence in absence; for example, my friend is absent only because in a certain sense he or she is also present to me. My mistake regarding his or her empirical presence does not negate his or her presence in absence. Each of us is situated in the world not simply in geographic space, but also in human space. Though my friend is several thousand miles away and is absent as an object, he or she can be present to me as a subject through whose look I become an object. Though the other-as-object may be at a distance from me in geographic space, the road(s) leading from myself to this other-as-object—that is, to my looking at the other—must be understood in terms of "instrumental complexes which allow me to cause an Other-as-object to appear as a 'this' on the ground of the world, an Other-as-object who is already implicitly and really contained there" (p. 279).[15] However, not only am I situated in human space in relation to specific others, but also to "every living man" (p. 279). And while I can be mistaken regarding the empirical presence of a look of an other, I cannot be wrong about the feeling of being looked-at, which is an aspect of my human reality.

In short it is in relation to every living man that every human reality is present or absent on the ground of an original presence. This original presence can have meaning only as a being-looked-at or as a being-looking-at. . . . Being-for-others is a constant fact of my human reality, and I grasp it with its factual necessity in every thought, however slight, which I form concerning myself. . . . The Other is present to me everywhere as the one through whom I become an object. [pp. 279–80]

Just how does a pre-reflective consciousness, which cannot be an object to itself, manage to feel the presence of the other when that other is not empirically present? One might say that consciousness can feel this presence because there has been an internalization of the other, in a process that eventually leads to the development of what Mead calls the generalized other. In having learned to take the role of the other, one can be both subject and object. But Sartre categorically asserts that pre-reflective consciousness cannot be its own object and maintains that it is the experience of the look, of being made to have an "outside," that convinces one of the other's existence.[16] Yet when he is forced to account for the presence of the

15. Sartre describes human beings as situated in "hodological" space, to use Kurt Lewin's term. "It refers to a map or spatial organization of our environment in terms of our acts and needs" (*BN*, p. 279n., translator's note).

16. If there is any doubt regarding the level of consciousness on which Sartre would place Mead's generalized other or Freud's superego, an interview with Leo Fretz held in 1976 is quite to the point. In the interview, Fretz has just mentioned to Sartre the example from *Being and Nothingness* of the homosexual who confesses his homosexuality to himself. (Note that the word *non-reflective* here refers to what has previously been termed *pre-reflective*.)

FRETZ: You adduce as an argument that the homosexual in the latter case is looking at himself. But if he is looking at himself, as you say, is his self not then constituted by an interiorized other, and can one not say, that this self is already a super-ego which is constituted by the other? SARTRE: Yes, that might be so in certain cases. But

non-empirical other, Sartre appeals to a fundamental being-for-others to ground the non-empirical experience. What are we to make of this appeal to a fundamental human reality that is present even when particular others are absent, if one of the major goals of an analysis of the look is to refute solipsism? Sartre starts from the cogito, from individual consciousness, but must acknowledge our being-for-others if solipsism is to be overcome.

At this juncture it seems appropriate to compare Sartre with Mead, who, instead of attempting to arrive at the social from the cogito, sought to show how a cogito arises from social relationships involving individual biological organisms and their symbolic interaction.

---

in fact the viewing of oneself by oneself, that is, the reflective consciousness which views the series of non-reflected moments of consciousness, in general merely supplies syntheses that are too simple; with parts that are ejected and crowded out, with continuities that are sharper or less sharp than in non-reflected consciousness. In brief, it provides primarily an object that is poorly constituted, that strives too much towards unity, that is too synthetic. It does not supply the truth of the non-reflected consciousness.

Jean-Paul Sartre and Leo Fretz, "An Interview with Jean-Paul Sartre," in *Jean-Paul Sartre—Contemporary Approaches to His Philosophy*, Eds. Hugh J. Silverman and Frederick A. Elliston, pp. 230–31.

CHAPTER THREE

Mead and Sartre

Comparison and Critique

ALTHOUGH THE APPROACHES AND CONCLUSIONS OF MEAD AND Sartre exhibit marked contrasts—for example, regarding the origin and nature of (self-) consciousness—these differences are moderated by shared claims and assumptions. Both reject traditional idealistic, rationalistic, mechanistic, and materialistic approaches to philosophical issues, while at the same time it is fair to say that each has a distinctive non-theistic idealistic strain in his thought. Contingency, novelty, and chance are crucial for each. For Mead, we must refer back to the "world that is there," and, for Sartre, to the existential in which novelty and contingency make sport of positions that neatly categorize and organize reality. Both see some form of non-reflective consciousness serving as the ground from which reflection springs, or comes to be; for each, there is no soul, substance, or self behind consciousness, because the self is an object of consciousness.

Nevertheless, the differences are striking. Even where there is apparent agreement on certain crucial points—for instance, the self as an object of consciousness—opposite conclusions are often drawn. The *true* self is cognitive for Mead, whereas for Sartre, the self that is cognitively known is the result of impure reflection and lends itself to bad faith and *inauthenticity*. In *Being and Nothingness* Sartre organizes his perspective from the cogito and claims to provide a phenomenological description of consciousness. Mead would shun this approach as being the stepchild of introspective psychology and, as such, non-scientific. The empirical social sciences provide the important insights for Mead, whereas for Sartre

science is the route of determinism and is often a source of bad
faith, especially in the case of the so-called psychological sciences.
Having looked at several very general points of comparison, we
will now review elements of their positions with a view to a more
detailed comparison. This will prepare the way for then showing
the inadequacies, as well as the strengths, of their respective approaches to the self and consciousness.

In taking the role of the other I come to view my responses from
the perspective of the other, according to Mead. In so doing, I learn
to view myself (my responses) as an object, and I develop a reflective consciousness. When the object that I am viewing is readily
seen from the perspective of the generalized other, I am fully self-
conscious. I now have a self in the form of an object that comes
into being when I reflect. For Sartre, on the other hand, I am never
simply my role, and in not being my role while being it I exhibit
the freedom of human consciousness. That I can never be my role
is due to the nature of consciousness; consciousness, whether reflective or pre-reflective, is what it is precisely by not being the object of which it is aware. When I see an object, I immediately experience consciousness as being aware of an object that appears to
it, an object, however, that is not itself consciousness. In Sartrean
terms, I am separated from the object by nothing, and this nothing
is consciousness. Further, consciousness is always nihilating; that
is, it is always distancing itself from what it was just aware of,
either by moving from the pre-reflective to the reflective level and
making pre-reflective consciousness into an object, and/or by having the focus of consciousness shifted as something appears to consciousness, in its nihilating activity, as different from what just appeared. This nihilating tendency of consciousness can be spoken of
as its temporality—to be what it is not and to not be what it is—
in the sense that one might speak of the vanishing "now" of time.
When I am playing a role in the present, my consciousness of the
role distances me from the role as it flees the present. Sartre con-
cludes from this that one is never simply a role. Yet, one plays a
role, and it is, in part, the pressure brought to bear by a powerful
"public" that leads one to act in this manner. To return to the
waiter,

The waiter in the café plays with his condition in order to *realize* it. This
obligation is not different from that which is imposed on all tradesmen.

Their condition is wholly one of ceremony. The public demands of them that they realize it as a ceremony. . . . Society demands that he limit himself to his function as a grocer. . . . There are indeed many precautions to imprison a man in what he is. . . .

Furthermore we are dealing with more than mere social positions; I am never any one of my attitudes, any one of my actions. [*BN*, pp. 59–60; original emphasis]

For Sartre, this public or other attempts to make me into a thing, an in-itself, to deny my transcendence. For Mead, however, it is the very process of role-taking that is responsible for providing me with the only self available to me. Nevertheless, Sartre and Mead seem not to be far apart in defining the self that role-taking provides; for both, it is an object-self. But in this definition Mead would appeal to a generalized other to round out the picture, claiming that specific roles are insufficient for producing an object-self. Sartre recognizes that there is indeed a "they" who can turn one into an object, and who can look at one even when not empirically present. However, this being-for-others, as a presence in absence, is a lurking presence that is ready to transform the selfness of consciousness into an in-itself by denying the transcendence of consciousness, denying the existence of nothing, which separates and holds apart, that is, denying *nothing* in favor of *being*. Without nothing, there is no freedom, but only the determinism found in the relationships between things that are connected causally. And causality does not allow room for "nothing" to deny its Parmenidian continuity.

Yet Sartre is well aware of the importance of the other. My being is a being-for-others and requires a me-as-object to become uniquely human. Without the me-as-object the distinction between my self(ness) and the other would evaporate because of our shared mode of being.[1] The me-as-object is the limit in which I maintain the consciousness of my selfness as not the selfness of the other. "I can not *not-be* the Other unless I assume my being-as-object for the Other. The disappearance of the alienated Me would involve the disappearance of the Other through the collapse of Myself" (*BN*, p. 285; original emphasis). We find that the for-itself, which the

1. *BN*, pp. 285–87; see also ch. 2 above.

other transforms into an object through the look, requires the me-as-object to maintain itself as "this" nothing, "this" consciousness.

Sartre claims that one cannot deduce ontologically the other from the for-itself, though the presence of the other cannot be denied by the for-itself. It is a fact that there are others.[2] Once the presence of the other is admitted, and once it is also recognized that the other shares my mode of being as consciousness—presumably because only another consciousness could look at me and rob me of my subjectivity—the problem arises regarding how I can establish and maintain my distance from the other. There are actually two interconnected, but different, issues at stake here, which Sartre tends to confuse: there is the issue of how I can keep the other at bay, and then there is the issue of how it comes about that I differentiate from an other who shares my mode of being. In both cases Sartre appeals to the concept of me-as-object, as a concept of limit, in order to characterize the processes involved. His account conflates the question of the genesis of this particular consciousness with the question of the maintenance of this consciousness in the face of a (hostile) consciousness.

The source of differentiation from the other—both in terms of genesis and maintenance—that the look gives rise to, that is, the me-as-object, must somehow both be and not be due to my consciousness. If it were solely due to my consciousness, this would mean that I could limit myself, be a finite totality, which Sartre holds I cannot be. Nor can I turn to the in-itself for the me-as-object, because the in-itself cannot limit consciousness due to its radical difference from consciousness; as Sartre tells us, only consciousness can limit consciousness (BN, pp. 286–87). Sartre's solution is to appeal to one's being-for-others, to the acceptance by consciousness of the object that it has been made into by the look of the other. This me-as-object must be me, for it is my "outside," my "nature." But it is also not me, in that my consciousness is immediately aware that it is not its object in its nihilation of the

2. "Being-for-others is not an ontological structure of the For-itself. We can not think of deriving being-for-others from a being-for-itself as one would derive a consequence from a principle, nor conversely can we think of deriving being-for-itself from being-for-others. . . . What the *cogito* reveals to us here is just factual necessity: it is found—and this is indisputable—that our being along with its being-for-itself is also for others" (BN, p. 282; original emphasis).

object. I am differentiated and saved from the other, but the price I pay for my salvation is to be me only by not being me.

I must accept the me-as-object in order to not be it, to reject it. I play at a role, which can only be a role, because the other sees me in the role. Yet once conscious of the role, I am no longer simply the role. I can use my awareness to escape the other. (A reflective agonist might say, "The other thinks I am only a so and so; little does he or she know me; watch now how I make sport of the other's image of me.") We must all be actors and actresses if we are to retain our freedom, but it is a negative freedom, a freedom of not being something or someone, of not being the role one is playing.

Sartre seeks to overcome solipsism with his analysis of the look, but if we are to overcome solipsism in this manner, we must be able to recognize the look of the other as a human look, as opposed to, for instance, the look of a baboon, a snake, or a cow. Of course, the possibility of recognition implies that we are not radically other to the human other, and, in fact, Sartre claims that we share a mode of being with the other, as previously mentioned. However, while he is well aware of the necessity of the other's existence for consciousness to be *human* consciousness, he is also convinced of the irrevocable otherness of the other, claiming that the other does not alter the ontology of individual consciousness.

Being-for-others is not an ontological structure of the For-itself. We can not think of deriving being-for-others from a being-for-itself. . . . Of course our human-reality must of necessity be simultaneously for-itself and for-others, but our present investigation does not aim at constituting an anthropology. It would perhaps not be impossible to conceive of a For-itself which would be wholly free from all For-others and which would exist without even suspecting the possibility of being an object. But this For-itself simply would not be "man." [BN, p. 282]

Sartre's argument is not convincing. If the me-as-object is as fundamental as his account suggests, then it is difficult to understand how we can avoid the language of ontology. Doesn't having a "nature," in the form of a me-as-object, imply that the other has become a part of (self-) consciousness? Consciousness, it would seem, cannot be merely the transparent nothing that Sartre describes if it depends on the other in order to not be the other, that is, to be itself. Must Sartre not be speaking of a nothing that is permeated by being, given that the being of the other has insinuated its way into the nothing by requiring consciousness to take hold of it in the form of the me-as-object (in order to have a limit from the other)? Has the other's presence not been internalized, to use an anti-Sartrean concept?

Mead would answer the latter questions in the affirmative, not only because being and non-being "interpenetrate" to produce a universe filled with change and novelty (*PP*, p. 1), but, more to the point, because we cannot understand mind and self-consciousness unless we understand that the other must in some sense be a part of self-consciousness. Sartre, on the other hand, must avoid the notion of an internalized other, for such an other would be a threat to the freedom and spontaneity of consciousness. It can be argued, nevertheless, that his account of the look suggests that the individual has permanently internalized the other due to the fact that one can become an object for an other who is not empirically present. Sartre, of course, rejects internalization as an explanation of this phenomenon, because consciousness would then be divided into consciousness and the object of which it is aware (that is, itself) on the pre-reflective level; in other words, the pre-reflective consciousness of the look would be transformed into a reflective consciousness.[3]

Instead of appealing to internalization to explain the feeling of being looked-at when no other is empirically present, might Sartre appeal to certain situations (for example, walking in dark alleys)? Occasions, rather than an internalized other, would then be said to create the feeling of objecthood. For Sartre, however, occasions for experiencing the look are simply that, occasions; underlying them is a more fundamental experience of being looked-at.

I can indeed believe that it is a man who is watching me in the half light and discover that it is a trunk of a tree which I took for a human being; my fundamental presence to all men, the presence of all men to myself is not thereby altered. For the appearance of a man as an object in the field of my experience is not what informs me that *there are* men. My certainty of the Other's existence is independent of these experiences and is, on the contrary, that which makes them possible. [*BN*, p. 280; original emphasis]

3. Cf. above, ch. 2, n. 16.

The look is transferred from the realm of specific encounters with others or specific occasions for being mistaken about the other's presence to a realm of human reality in general. The reason we can feel looked-at when no one else is empirically present is that we are always in some way for-others.

We are able now to apprehend the nature of the look. In every look there is the appearance of an Other-as-object as a concrete and probable presence in my perceptive field; on the occasion of certain attitudes of that Other I determine myself to apprehend—through shame, anguish, etc.— my being-looked-at. This "being-looked-at" is presented as the pure probability that I am at present this concrete *this*—a probability which can derive its meaning and its very nature as probable, only from a fundamental certainty that the Other is always present to me inasmuch as I am always *for-others*. [BN, pp. 280–81; original emphasis]

If one can be mistaken regarding a specific look of an other, then it would appear that *a* look can no longer serve as the concrete proof that it first appeared to be of the other's existence. It now seems that any specific look entails a probable appearance of the other, whose existence we now "know" is certain only because our own reality is a being-for-others. Yet, Sartre claims, being-for-others finds its proof concretely realized "on the occasion of the upsurge of an object into *my* universe if this object indicates to me that I am probably an object at present functioning as a *differentiated this* for a consciousness" (*BN*, p. 281; original emphasis).[4] The introduction of the mistaken look forces Sartre to posit a permanent presence in absence for the other, which, in turn, relies on *a* look of an other for proof of this presence. As a refutation of solipsism this circularity will not do. Further, the introduction of the non-empirical presence of the other raises critical questions. Given Sartre's claims regarding the radical freedom of consciousness, how can he account for the fact that the presence of the absent other is felt more deeply in some contexts than others? Experience reveals that, even when the other is not empirically present, different circumstances, for example, dark alleys, affect different individ-

---

4. Sartre goes on to say that "the proof is the ensemble of the phenomenon which we call the *look*. Each look makes us prove concretely—and in the indubitable certainty of the *cogito*—that we exist for all living men" (p. 281; original emphasis).

uals in different ways in terms of the feeling of being looked-at. Why should this be so, and how can Sartre's model account for it? Why should specific non-empirical looks be more potent than others?

An internalized other could conceivably explain both the existence and the power of the absent other, but to speak in terms of internalization of the other is to risk the loss of the radical freedom that Sartre takes to be so basic to consciousness. If consciousness contains an internalized other in some shape or form, then it is not pure translucence but tainted, for the other can convert consciousness into an object from within. In this case, the other is no longer an external subject that sets the stage for accepting the me-as-object in order to escape the other, but is an aspect of consciousness that can make one feel looked-at, turned into an object, even when the other is not empirically present.

In discussing a section of *Being and Nothingness* in 1976, Sartre appears to argue that if the interiorized other has any impact on consciousness, it is on the reflective level of consciousness and not on the pre-reflective.[5] Perhaps there is some truth to this claim, and the internalized other is to be found in the sphere of reflective consciousness. But if this is so, how is Sartre's pre-reflective look of the absent other to be explained, given the problems previously mentioned? After a brief discussion of Mead's position on reflection, I will utilize his perspective to argue that the look's transformation of oneself into an object is in fact a phenomenon of reflective consciousness, one that *only appears* to take place on the pre-reflective level.

Mead's strength lies in providing an account of just how the outside other comes to be inside through the verbal gesture, role-taking, and the development of the generalized other. In Mead's view, the self comes into being as one's responses and roles are seen from the perspective of the other and the generalized other, and reflection is crucial in this development. It is only by turning to view one's responses from the perspective of the other and the, or a, generalized other, that one comes to have a self.

Mead, however, does not appear to appreciate the importance of what Sartre calls pre-reflective (self-) consciousness. For Mead,

5. See above, ch. 2, n. 16.

there is reflective consciousness in which the self appears as an object (corresponding to Sartre's impure reflection), and there is a
non-self-consciousness in which one responds without thinking
about one's responses. For example, I drive down a road that I have
driven down many times; I arrive at my house from my friend's
house and wonder where I have been during the trip, for my self
seems to have been absent. I know in retrospect that it must have
been me who drove home, and that I must have made appropriate
responses while doing so without reflecting on my self, that is, I
must have responded without at all being aware of my self. Though
Mead discusses non-reflective experiences of this type as well as
reflective consciousness, he is insensitive to the level of awareness
in which one has a *sense of self* without making the self into an
object. For Sartre, consciousness has a sense of itself as a diasporic
unity on this level, and this sense of self is not the self encountered
as an object of study in "scientific" psychological approaches.

Mead is not totally unaware of the issue. Although he does not
speak in terms of a sense of self or of an indirect awareness of self
on the pre-reflective level, he does attempt to account for a "running current of awareness of what we do which is distinguishable
from the consciousness of the field of stimulation."[6] In other words,
Mead is sensitive to the fact that we often feel as if we are not only
aware of objects but also aware of the consciousness (or subject)
that is aware of objects, without explicitly making this consciousness into an object. However, Mead does not think that the awareness, the "I," can ever have an awareness of itself. One can only be
aware of objects, or the object-self, the "me." The so-called "running current of awareness" does not provide a direct intuition of
an "I" that is aware. It is due to a new "I's" awareness of my response to my own (or another's) stimulus; it is the original "me,"
my original response or set of responses acting as a stimulus, and
"commented on" by a new "me."[7] The sense of self, as consciousness immediately (albeit, indirectly) aware of itself, is actually an
illusion; it is in reality an object-self produced by the rapidity with
which one learned to respond both to others and to oneself through
the verbal gesture.

6. Mead, *SS*, p. 144.
7. *SS*, p. 145. See ch. 1 above for a more detailed discussion.

I will argue in Part Two that Mead is incorrect in limiting consciousness to non-reflective and reflective levels. But Sartre is wrong when he claims that the non-empirical look of the other takes place on the pre-reflective level of consciousness, and Mead's account of the "running current of awareness" serves as a key to understanding Sartre's confusion. Before discussing how Mead would explain the non-empirical look, however, we should consider how Mead would address Sartre's account of the look in which there is an other empirically present.

Mead would argue that there is indeed some truth to be found in Sartre's presentation of how the me-as-object—that is, the self-as-object—comes into being through the look of the other. In Sartre's terms, I must accept (as well as reject) the me-as-object that the other produces by looking at me; Mead, on the other hand, would claim that it is only by looking at myself from the perspective of the other than I come to have an object-self at all. But Sartre's description is needlessly abstract, presenting only clues to a complex developmental process that extends over a number of years. For Mead, becoming an object-self involves considerably more than being looked-at by an other. I must learn to respond to myself through the verbal gesture; I must then go on to take the role of the other and generalized other(s). In so doing, I come to view myself (without the empirical presence of the other) from various perspectives; I come to be both subject and object to myself. When, as in Sartre's account, the (empirical) other appears and looks at me, I am moved to view myself from the perspective of that other, as I have done so many times in the past during my development as a self. I see myself as a "me" from the other's perspective, and this seeing entails a feeling of immediacy due to the actual presence and attitude of the other (who is "playing the role" of subject). Certain looks—such as a scoffing glance—imply that I am merely a specific set of behaviors or qualities, and when I meet them I feel as if my freedom has been stolen from me. I feel this way because the "I," which responds more or less spontaneously to the world and to the "me," has been (temporarily) captured by the other. I see myself as the other forces me to see myself. That the other can so force me is due to the fact that my development as an object-self has required that I learn how and when to respond to different attitudes of the other, attitudes that reveal and are revealed in the look of the other.

Even Sartre recognizes the importance of these attitudes when he states that

> we are able now to apprehend the nature of the look. In every look there is the appearance of an Other-as-object as a concrete and probable presence in my perceptive field; on the occasion of certain attitudes of that Other I determine myself to apprehend—through shame, anguish, etc.— my being-looked-at. [BN, pp. 280–81]

Sartre would note that it is more accurate to say that I do not become an object to myself, but that I become an object for the other when looked-at by the other. And there is a truth to this in that one is an object for the other before one develops an object-self through taking the role of the other. (What it would feel like to be an object under such circumstances, that is, before the object-self comes into being, Mead cannot say.) For Mead, objectness does not remain out there in the world, so to speak; it becomes a part of one's consciousness as the object-self develops. Be this as it may, Sartre's claim that I must in some way accept the me-as-object as my own, and his conviction that I can experience the look when the other is not empirically present, challenge the accuracy and comprehensiveness of his contention that I am not an object to myself but remain an object for the other (with regard to the look).

As we have seen, Sartre's own claims regarding the non-empirical look of the other call into question his presentation of the look as a phenomenon of pre-reflective consciousness. The reason that it appears to take place on the pre-reflective level can be found in Mead's explanation of how we can believe that we are aware of the observer "I" without transforming it into an object, namely, that in speaking (to myself or to others), I hear myself through the verbal gesture and respond. The speech, the response, and consciousness of the response often appear to take place at almost the same instant, yielding a "running current of awareness" and the impression that I am a subject directly aware of myself. When I feel as if I am being watched, even though there is no other empirically present, I am making an object of myself. I am taking the attitude of the other toward myself. However, I am responding to myself so rapidly that I do not perceive my response, and my becoming conscious of it, as due to my own abilities, abilities which I have developed through years of symbolic interaction. I thus feel *as if* I am being watched by someone else on a pre-reflective level, though in reality I am responding (and becoming conscious of my response) to a given stimulus, a stimulus that does not require the empirical presence of the other. Given the fact that each of us has a different developmental history, certain situations (for example, dark alleys), actions, or thoughts, will call out for each of us especially potent looks (responses) from the past—a past in which it was learned that specific behaviors call out marked and rapid responses from others. Thus, while rapidity of response is a necessary condition for the possibility of confusing pre-reflective and reflective experience, it is our individual histories that account for the circumstances under which the confusion occurs.

I would again like to stress that, although I have argued that Sartre is wrong regarding the *level* of consciousness at which the look's transformation of oneself into an object takes place, I am not—following Mead—willing to limit consciousness to reflective and non-reflective levels. I am convinced that an indirect, pre-reflective consciousness of self exists, and that Mead's model cannot adequately deal with it and is thus in need of modification. I will discuss these latter assertions later in this chapter and in Part Two. I should also add that although the look is a phenomenon of reflective consciousness, it is also true that one can begin to *feel* what becomes the look of the other before one is fully cognizant of being an object. And this can only be explained if pre-reflective consciousness and its relationship to reflection are properly understood.

Mead's suggestion for dealing with the (mistaken) sense we have of being aware of the "I" is of assistance in interpreting the look; nonetheless, his approach to this and other questions of self and consciousness is beset with numerous difficulties. The subject–object dichotomy on which his model hinges sees the self as merely an object, and only because the self is an object can it be whole, in his view. This wholeness, or completeness, arises because one comes to view oneself from the perspective of the generalized other (*MSS*, pp. 144, 154–55). However, if the wholeness that Mead attributes to the self is only the wholeness of an object viewed as a totality, how are we to understand the relationship that this whole has to the subject that is aware of it and responds to it? We might, following one of Mead's suggestions, think of the "I," the subject, as a necessary presupposition, a fiction of sorts, for there can only be an object if there is a subject (*SS*, p. 142). But Mead also argues that the "I" is the sphere of novel responses which the organism makes to itself and the world. Having begun by treating the "I" and the "me" solely as functional distinctions, he must come to terms with their metaphysical implications if novelty is to be seen as a real aspect of the person and the world, and if the object-self is to be the totality that novelty transforms. Yet, if we accept the metaphysical reality of the "I" as the sphere of novelty, we are left with an aspect of the person that can never be known. To know the "I" is impossible, for one can only know the "me," that the "I" becomes as the object of another "I," as the stream of consciousness moves on. As soon as the "I" is observed, it has already lost its status as an "I" and become a "me." The person, as a composite of "I" and "me," is caught in a dualism that leads to an infinite regress regarding self-knowledge.

The integration of the novel with the existent "me" is understood by Mead in terms of the principle of sociality, so that the change from the old "me" to the new "me" entails the change from an old system to a new one. Even so, it is still the case that the new self that arises from the encounter with the novel is an object-self, which cannot be known until the novel has been integrated with the original "me" in the production of a new me-system (*SS*, p. 148). We are left with a self that is an object in what Sartre would call impure reflection; and, a sense of self—perhaps as a current of awareness—is illusory because consciousness can never grab hold of an "I" that is aware of objects. What this in turn suggests is that the self is not, and cannot be, responsible for the integration of novelty; the integration goes on behind, or outside, the self as an object. If there is unity to the self, it is the unity of a "thing," of an object, albeit a very complex object. If there is spontaneity, it is a spontaneity that happens to the self, for the person may contain a pole of novelty, but the self does not and cannot. The self, it seems, cannot shape its own destiny. It is not free to rebel against its own past.

Is it not misleading to say that the self is not spontaneous or the home of novelty? After all, for Mead the person, or personality, has the poles of the "I" and the "me," which means that the organism can act in a spontaneous manner and is capable of rejecting its past in favor of the novel, even if the self cannot.[8] But what is at stake here is not whether the person or the self does or does not "contain" spontaneity or novelty; what is critical is whether the person or self can have any self-conscious control over what he or she becomes. The novel happens to the "me." The self cannot decide to incorporate the novel, nor can the "I," which can act in a spontaneous and novel fashion, by itself reflect on how it will act. The "I" may be creating or implementing new responses, and it may be aware of what is happening, but unless there is a self present, there is no reflection on what is happening. The self is found already constituted, and though the manner in which it is constituted must play a part in what the "I" does, it cannot direct or determine the "I." There is no place in Mead's model for freedom, if freedom is understood as entailing the capacity for self-conscious selection of who or what one wishes to become, the conscious making of the self or person by the self. Though Mead emphasizes the importance of reflective intelligence in shaping the (human) world, an "I" only becomes cognitively aware of changes to the self once the changes have already taken place and have been assimilated to a "me." Freedom as self-determination (at minimum) would require not only the capacity to change, to be different from what one has been in the past, but to have some conscious control over the change, to have a "self-knowledge" while the change is taking shape. We will return to the question of the nature of a self-determining self and the suitability of Mead's model to deal with this toward the end of this chapter and in chapter 4.

Mead's model cannot adequately account for the indirect awareness of self that occurs on the pre-reflective level. This is because he has sharply divided consciousness into reflective and non-reflective components, placing the weight of reflection at the object pole of consciousness. Sartre would claim that the key to freedom lies on the pre-reflective level, where the "self" is not an object, not a thing, but still has a sense of itself as one who acts.

According to Mead, as noted, one can never be directly aware of the awareness that is conscious of the "me." Sartre would agree, insofar as there is no soul or ego to be found aware of itself. Con-

8. For clarification of the distinction between personality and self, see ch. 1 above, n. 18.

sciousness, pre-reflective consciousness, must be its own (diasporic) unity if it is not to be lost, lost, that is, as discontinuous moments of awareness. For Sartre, it is not the ego as an object in a reflective consciousness that personalizes consciousness, that gives it a sense of self, a sense of unity. "The Ego is far from being the personalizing pole of a consciousness . . . it is consciousness in its fundamental selfness which under certain conditions allows the appearance of the Ego as the transcendent phenomenon of that selfness" (*BN*, p. 103). The very nature of consciousness is to be a dispersed unity, to be the constant nihilation of itself, "to be what it is not and to not be what it is," and as such it is thoroughly temporal. Though there is no foundation for the unity of consciousness behind consciousness, a quasi-unity is produced as the moments of consciousness nihilate themselves and are related to themselves in this nihilation. There is, then, no need for Sartre to appeal to an unconscious to unify consciousness.

Consciousness is present to itself, and in Sartre's view, this presence is based upon the ekstatic character of consciousness. Presence entails an ideal self which is different from the awareness of self that arises in impure reflection. The ideal self is experienced as the *limit* of the awareness of pre-reflective consciousness, as consciousness continually nihilates the consciousness that it is. Consciousness is an open totality which has as its horizon the limit of its own awareness. Yet, if this is all there were to the pre-reflective self, one might wish to characterize it as simply the (ideal) limit of awareness for a consciousness that is thoroughly temporal. But Sartre tells us that consciousness, in its flight from itself, is also referred to itself in terms of its possibilities: "What one is in the form of lack constitutes selfness or the second aspect of the person" (*BN*, p. 104).

The awareness of possibilities defines what one is in terms of what one is not, what one lacks. That which one lacks gives rise to one's sense of self. I become aware of myself as that which lacks x, y, or z. Further, this lack, this not being or having x, y, or z, relates the pre-reflective self to itself as that which can choose x, y, or z. Existence precedes essence. My possibilities reveal what my essence can be, depending on what I choose. So we find the above quotation followed by: "In fact how can the person be defined if not as a free relation to himself?" (*BN*, p. 104).

This freedom marks the human being as a subject, as the creature

who is aware of having freedom. Note, though, that we are discussing here pre-reflective consciousness; one does not have to
move to the level of reflection to be aware of, or have present, one's
possibilities, to have a sense of self. Consciousness itself provides
the sense of self by continually being aware that it is the awareness
that has these possibilities before it. The importance of choice in
Sartre's philosophical orientation is grounded in his model of pre-
reflective consciousness, for at every moment consciousness has
open to it possibilities whose appearance necessitates decision, and
by these choices the subject continually creates itself.

As we have noted, Sartre views consciousness as the nothing that
engages in the nihilation of itself and of objects of which it is aware.
As the upsurge of nothing, consciousness is continually separating
from itself. It is born anew at each moment. As a spontaneity, it
appears to create *ex nihilo*. Yet Sartre is also well aware of the fact
that consciousness is present to itself and has a sense of itself as a
(quasi-) unity. Consciousness is able to retain its quasi-unity in the
face of its self-nihilation because it can see itself in terms of what it
lacks, of what it could be, of what it is not, of what it desires, of
what is not-self; continuity lies in not being (and often desiring) x,
y, or z.

However, in pursuing the implications of Sartre's position, we see
that the tables are turned on his claim that consciousness is a spontaneity. In not being x or y, in lacking x or y, consciousness not only
nihilates an object; in this case it nihilates a unique object, that is,
what it specifically lacks. The possibilities that are not-me, not-self,
are my possibilities by virtue of being seen as what I am not but
could become, and the experience of what I am not must make
reference to what I am, my current being. When met by my nihilating consciousness, these possibilities do not merely maintain (as
other objects would) their negative relation to consciousness; my
consciousness actively chooses to deny the negative relation by
seeking to realize specific possibilities for itself through the negation of what is not-self. And, it must be able to succeed, to some
degree, if the notion of choice is to have any meaning at all.

The seeming ability of consciousness to create ex nihilo is an
illusion: first, because it comes to relate in an affirmative way to
what it is not, what it lacks, by overcoming the lack in realizing its
possibilities; second, because the nihilations of consciousness by
themselves are not external to themselves in the way in which He-

gel's account of time in the *Philosophy of Nature* (at first) suggests that negativity is external to itself.[9] The nihilations of consciousness differ from the nihilations of random objects in the world, for each nihilation directly relates to that which came before, and only becomes what it is by having a negative relation to it. This cannot be an external negative relation, because if each nihilation were merely external to the other nihilations, there would be only discontinuous moments, which could not possibly yield a sense of self. The nihilations must be gathered together by the very process in which they engage, so that (a) consciousness does not arise purely spontaneously but in relation to itself in the negation of itself. I should note in passing that I do not mean to suggest that Sartre does not make a distinction between the nihilations of objects and those of consciousness itself, only that he does not see or accept the dialectical implications of his model for his claim of spontaneity. Consciousness defined as "nothing," as nihilations, can be a unity and have a sense of self because its moments relate to each other by nihilating each other *and* because they have the "corporate" project of negating what consciousness lacks, what is not-self.

Mead is convinced of the importance of the novel, the unique, but relies on the conservative "me" to explain the basic nature of the self, that is, to be an object of the generalized other. While his account of consciousness is inadequate, being devoid of prereflective consciousness and the sense of self that exists at this level, his principle of sociality can be used to clarify the nature of the prereflective sense of self described by Sartre.

Mead sees sociality as a way of discussing the movement from an old system to a new one. He views the self as a system, and as a cognitive phenomenon, that comes to be and know itself as a system of behaviors by taking the role of the other. "If anything is comprehensible it is because of its relation to some other entity or entities in a system. Without presupposing a system, nothing could be thought about; nothing would have significance, since nothing by itself (such as a particular) has significance."[10] Sociality tells us that there is a betwixt-and-between systems in which a novel occurrence brings forth a readjustment in the system it affects, so that a new system arises. The novel makes us reinterpret what has been

9. See ch. 2 above.
10. Miller, *George Herbert Mead*, p. 189.

because we then view the past in light of the present new system. If we speak in causal terms, we may, for example, find causes for the new in the old, causes that we did not realize were there (and indeed were not there) until the novel arose to bring about the new system.

Before moving on to discuss the self and the sense of self in terms of sociality and novelty, I should pause to address the metaphysical implications of Mead's position. Mead is well aware that the absolutely novel would have no lasting place in the universe, for it could not be integrated into any system due to its radical difference. For example, a genetic mutation bearing little relation to its environment could not survive. Does not the claim that there must be some similarity between the so-called novel event and the (old) system (which it alters in giving rise to a new system), lead us into the relational and systemic universe of Spinoza or Hegel? In other words, if there must be some relationship between the novel and the old system, can we speak of the novel as radically new, and if not, is not everything ultimately related in one totalizing system? Can one think in terms of systems, as Mead does, without eventually being forced to regard the universe as a single system in which pure novelty is as unacceptable as the proposition that something can come from nothing?[11]

It is worth noting that even Hegel, who declares the Whole to be the Truth, is convinced, in contrast to Spinoza, that novelty and contingency exist; for him, it is the impotence of nature in not fully actualizing the Idea that lies behind this contingency and that leads to the existence of abominations and mutations in nature.[12] Be this as it may, this is not the place to answer the metaphysical question

11. In *PP* Mead, as we saw in ch. 1, rejects a metaphysics that would deny the novel and emergent. In *MSS* he states: "This brings out the general question as to whether anything novel can appear. Practically, of course, the novel is constantly happening and the recognition of this gets its expression in more general terms in the concept of emergence. Emergence involves a reorganization, but the reorganization brings in something that was not there before. The first time oxygen and hydrogen come together, water appears" (p. 198).

12. "This is the impotence of nature, that it cannot adhere to and exhibit the strictness of the Notion [*Begriff*] and runs wild in this blind irrational (*begrifflos*) multiplicity. . . . The Notion is absolute power just because it can freely abandon its difference to the shape of self-subsistent diversity, outer necessity, contingency, caprice, opinion, which however must not be taken for more than the abstract aspect of *nothingness*" (Hegel, *Science of Logic*, 607–08; original emphasis).

of the ultimate status of novelty. We can sidestep the issue for Mead here. First, we can limit his metaphysical claims regarding the status of the novel (found in *PP*) by speaking of novelty in terms of events that can qualitatively alter the organization of what can be spoken of as a system (for example, as we saw in chapter 1, the life in and around a pond is a system, and by introducing a new species one can alter the ecology). Second, given the thrust of our interest in Mead's work, namely, self and self-determination, I think it is fair to assume that there are events which are novel in social-psychological terms—that is, events that are sufficiently different from what the self or individual has experienced in its past to make them unique in relation to the individual (for example, contact with members of another culture). The uniqueness lies in the relationship between the self as a system of behaviors and behaviors that are new in relation to the established self system. Of course, this does not answer the metaphysical question, nor does it obviate other problems found in Mead's account of novelty and sociality in relation to the self, but it does allow us to engage Mead's approach, with the understanding that the focus of our interest lies in novelty of a social-psychological variety.

For Mead, reality is in the present, a present that refers to a hypothetical past and future.[13] The past is what it is in relation to the present and is found in the present, while the future looms as an extrapolation from the present. Mead argues that change or exchange of parts within a closed system should not be viewed as a temporal change, which implies that there is no temporality, and therefore no history, without the novel. From this it follows that only because there are both I- and me-poles can one self-consciously experience personal history. (For example, if there were but a me-pole, one would be solidified in a world without [personal] history, in a closed [self] system.)

Mead often uses the terms *system* and *perspective* interchangeably, because a system is a perspective, a way of marking off a set of relationships. Human reality involves a shifting of perspectives, which makes for new systems, new perspectives; one sees oneself as one has seen oneself in the past and then from the (new) perspective of the other. However, Mead does not carry his principle of sociality into the realm of pre-reflective consciousness. By this I

13. *PP*, p. 21; see also ch. 1 above.

mean to suggest that he fails to note that out of the viewing of oneself as an object, from the perspective of the other in reflective consciousness, there emerges a pre-reflective consciousness which has an indirect sense of itself because it lives (non-cognitively) its in-between-ness, its sociality.

The self as an object of cognition appears as a closed system, but consciousness repeatedly has thrust before it unique events and comes to expect and anticipate that such unforeseen possibilities will require living in sociality. Sociality is the standing between that which was and that which is coming to be, between the given and the new system that is set in motion by the novel, between the role I have taken and the unique response of the other (or myself) to this role (which, in turn, alters my self). Unlike the sociality of non-conscious events, for example, the assimilation of a mutation in an ecosystem, the consciousness that has experienced self-consciousness is thoroughly and consciously temporal. Again and again it adjusts to new responses from itself and its environment, especially its interpersonal environment. (Sartre would say that it is what it is not and is not what it is.) It is thoroughly temporal because it has had to develop the capacity to be itself while not being itself, in its confrontation with the novel.

I again wish to take issue with Mead's bifurcation of consciousness into reflective and non-reflective levels, because one can also have a non-objective sense of self on a pre-reflective level. One can have this sense of self because the constant "taking the role of the other" requires learning to adjust to the often unique responses of oneself and the other, leading to a pre-reflective anticipation of not being oneself. Consciousness becomes aware that it must confront what it is not, and it develops an orientation toward the future. Consciousness becomes temporal and has a sense of itself as the one who is responding, because it experiences not only the past, cognitively known object-self or the purely hypothetical future self, but the repeated transitions between object-self and the not (yet) self. It learns to live in between, in sociality.[14]

14. I by no means wish to suggest that the future is unimportant to Mead. The social act surely entails an anticipatory dimension, and thinking itself must be seen as teleological in that its primary purpose is to overcome difficulties. As Miller points out, "The function of mind is to direct conduct in the face of the uncertainties, and it always involves reference to what is not here-now, not in the specious present, not

I would also like to suggest along these lines that, Sartre notwithstanding, the pre-reflective sense of self is not prior to reflection—
something the pre-reflective is supposed to give rise to in its anguish
over its freedom—but follows the making of the self into an object,
that is, it is posterior to reflective consciousness. Sartre is correct in
saying that consciousness views itself in terms of what it lacks.
However, it can only lack because of its ability to take various perspectives on itself. The animal lacks nothing, for it craves only certain specific things in the immediacy of the moment, whereas human reality entails the freedom that arises from the consciousness
of not being or having x. This not being or having rests on a consciousness that can respond and view itself as other than itself, so
as to experience itself as lacking what the other has. Part Two will
clarify and defend these rather sketchy suggestions.

Mead, of course, not only bifurcates experience into the reflective
and non-reflective, but also into the "I" and the "me." In doing so
there seems to be no middle ground for a (self-) consciousness that
can process novel experiences as it is having them. We know that
the self is a system for Mead, that it is an object of cognition, and
that the novel as novel can have no place in the self until it has been
integrated into the me-system. As a particular event, the novel must
reside outside the self until its pure particularity has been overcome
by its relationship to other elements in the self system. This leaves
Mead's model in the awkward position of having the pole of novelty, the "I," which is also the pole of non-reflective awareness, appear as external to the self. Only when both the "I" and the "me"
are present is there reflective consciousness, so that if the "I" is
present without the "me," one cannot reflect. In other words, the
transition from an old me-system to a new me-system is never
under self-conscious guidance or control, for if a new response is
generated by the "I," the "I" cannot know this as it is happening.

---

in immediate experience. . . . Mind's function is to reconstruct action so that inhi-
bitions may be dispensed with" (*George Herbert Mead,* p. 40). My point, then, is
not that the future has no place in Mead's approach, but that the transitions of
sociality and the experience of the future, in terms of "what consciousness is not"
in the present, give rise to a pre-reflective (self-) consciousness. This consciousness is
not adequately addressed by Mead's bifurcation of consciousness into reflective and
non-reflective. A more detailed explanation of this claim is reserved for the next
chapter.

Is it really the case that (self-) consciousness of the novel only takes place upon reflection, that is, after the novel has been integrated into a self? Experience would seem to suggest that one can be aware of something as novel for oneself, while it is still novel and not yet integrated into the self; in other words, one can have a pre-reflective (self-) awareness of it before it has become an object (of study). For example, I walk into a room and I am struck by an odor, an odor that I have never smelled before and that is totally unanticipated. I am aware of the novelty of the odor as being novel to me before I reflect or comment on it. (When I do begin to reflect on it, I might then ask questions such as, What is it? Where and when have I smelled something like it in the past?) Unlike the experience of the look, in which I feel as if I am an object, there is a non-objective newness here that is prior to a specific act of reflection, and that cannot be accounted for by even the most rapidly responding reflective consciousness of Mead's "I" and "me" model. Reflection may be set in motion by the encounter, but the original experience is not the result of a specific act of reflection. On the other hand, it must be emphasized that the sense of newness here is for a particular consciousness; and the consciousness that is aware of it must live in a world of anticipation that the odor violates. In Part Two we will be looking at how this world of anticipation develops from *non*-reflective consciousness.

If, for Mead, self-consciousness comes in only after the response to the novel has already taken place, then freedom would appear to mean only that one is not determined in a mechanistic fashion, due to the existence of the I-pole of the personality. This is not a freedom in which one can self-consciously determine how the self develops, but simply a freedom in which one avoids a preordained self through the existence of novelty. On the other hand, Mead speaks of freedom in the *Philosophy of the Act* as something more than this; he speaks of it in terms of one's capacity for avoiding compulsion, for being and acting as a whole individual.

Compulsion disintegrates the individual into his different elements; hence there are degrees of freedom in proportion to the extent to which the individual becomes organized as a whole. It is not often that the whole of us goes into any act so that we face the situation as an entire personality. Moreover, this does not necessarily spell creation, spontaneity; it spells the identification of the individual with the act. Freedom, then, is the expression of the *whole self* which has become entire through the reconstruction which has taken place.[15]

This passage is from a section entitled "Miscellaneous Fragments," and was—as was the rest of the *Philosophy of the Act*—culled and edited after Mead's death. What is striking is that on first reading one might be inclined to say that Mead locates freedom for the individual *not* solely in the spontaneous "I," as previously suggested, but in the whole personality, both the "I" and the "me." However, we have already noted that Mead argues that the self as a whole can only be and be known as a social object, and given that the object pole of the self is clearly the me-pole, freedom on this reading would be associated with the "me" and not the "I," due to the emphasis on wholeness. If, on the other hand, Mead is *not* locating freedom in the "me," the part of the self that can be known as whole, but in the personality, which includes the "I" and the "me," then we are left with an extremely paradoxical situation. One is free when one's entire person acts as a whole, but one cannot and does not act as a reconstructed whole when one is disorganizing and reconstructing the old self with novel responses. Change involving novelty appears to run contrary to the wholeness of the reconstructed self, yet freedom without change would involve only the me-pole of the personality. In any case, it is safe to conclude that the dualism of the "I" and the "me" renders self-conscious self-determination a contradiction in terms for Mead, because the mechanism of change does not in itself entail reflection, and reflection is the only form of self-consciousness that Mead is prepared to accept.

Sartre, for whom freedom is at the heart of consciousness, denies the existence of an ego behind consciousness, and thus the ego, or self, becomes an object of reflective consciousness. As Sartre declares in *Nausea*, the self is a story we tell ourselves, a story that appears to have begun in the past but that actually begins at the end, in the present.[16] Though the present situation suggests, as it were, what past to create and accept, consciousness is free not to

15. Mead, *The Philosophy of the Act,* p. 663; emphasis added.
16. Sartre, *Nausea,* pp. 56–58.

be what it takes itself to be. It does not have to be any particular story; it can distance itself from the current self.

While there is no self behind consciousness, for Sartre there is a sense of self, a subjecthood, that one experiences in the present. Consciousness has a quasi-unity that is defined by the limit of pre-reflective consciousness and by its possibilities; and through this quasi-unity the subject avoids the utter nihilism that would result from unrelated nihilations of consciousness. Without (quasi-) unity, consciousness would have no reason to answer to itself, and Sartre's claims regarding responsibility would be rendered nonsensical. But on what grounds, from Sartre's standpoint, does a consciousness choose one future, one set of possibilities, over another? He cannot allow for choice by a self that instigates a particular choice, for to him the self is but an object of consciousness and, as radically free, consciousness does not answer to its objects. Why choose x over y? The only reason can be that what is chosen is deemed worthy of value by consciousness at the time of the choice, while the set of chosen and non-chosen possibilities define the parameters of consciousness's sense of self. This sense of self, which appears as a product of consciousness's present opening to its future, cannot self-consciously decide on one future over another, because it is being created in the flow of consciousness toward consciousness's possibilities. It is brought into existence by a consciousness that answers to nothing.

Neither Mead nor the early Sartre has an adequate account of self-determination, if self-determination is seen as entailing a capacity to direct the development of the self that one wishes to become, through self-consciously made choices in the present. Mead fails because in his model the self appears as determined and split off from the "I." Sartre's account of the sense of self provides the sensitivity to pre-reflective consciousness that is missing in Mead's position, but he cannot arrive at self-determination as long as he insists that the self is brought into being by a consciousness that is pure spontaneity. What is needed, then, is a synthesis of certain aspects of the positions of Mead and Sartre. To speak of the self is to speak of that which must in some way be unified, but if this unity is to be self-determining it must be capable of modifying itself. At the very least, it must not be a closed system, a mere object of cognition, but an open system, a system capable of sociality. Further, if Mead's insights regarding the development of self-consciousness are in the main correct, the other must play a vital role in the process of the self's development and in the development of the capacity for self-conscious self-determination. How, though, can one's relationships to others, which for both Sartre and Mead give rise to an object-self, be seen as giving rise to a subject capable of choosing its own future? In other words, how is it possible to explain the emergence of a free subject from a realm of determined objective roles and relationships? It is this question that we shall address in Part Two.

Part II

CHAPTER FOUR

From Mediated to Mediating Self

The Development of the Self-determining Self

Introduction

IN CHAPTER 3 I ARGUED THAT MEAD IS INSUFFICIENTLY SENSI-tive to the *sense of self* that exists on the pre-reflective level of consciousness, and that Sartre, though providing a description of this sense of self, cannot adequately account for the birth of consciousness and the development of reflective consciousness. The appearance of reflective consciousness, for Sartre, is due to the insecurity of pre-reflective consciousness—it fears its own spontaneity and, hence, attempts to arrest it. I suggested that the sense of self on the pre-reflective level actually arises after the development of reflective consciousness—that is, first one is an object to oneself, and only then can a (pre-reflective) sense of self arise. Now this suggestion may seem to fly in the face of so-called common sense, for is it not the case that before the baby has him or herself as an object, there is a world of pure pre-reflective experience? After Piaget, must we not agree that cognition proceeds through demonstrable phases of development? And this being so, is it not obvious that consciousness must develop its capacity to differentiate and reflect on objects and itself from a prior pre-reflective stage?

However, I do not mean to suggest that there is an absence of non-reflective experience prior to reflection, but that the (pre-reflective) consciousness that has a sense of self differs from the initial non-reflective experience of the infant. In this chapter I hope to show that non-reflective experience must be mediated by the development of reflective consciousness if a sense of self is to develop. Before the sense of self can become part of his or her pre-reflective consciousness, the child must learn to take various responses of others, "the role of the other," so as to become an object to him or her self. Until one can view oneself from the perspective of the other, there can be no awareness of oneself as one who has possibilities. In other words, the consciousness that makes so-called choices before it has a sense of self—for example, the young infant who reaches for one toy instead of another—is not the consciousness that chooses with reference to its own possibilities. In sum, the development of the self as a social object must precede the choice-making pre-reflective sense of self.

At this point, the reader may want to offer a seemingly obvious counterexample concerning the preferences and seeming awareness of possibilities that the (approximately) year-old child begins to exhibit in the form of a particular symbolic gesture. The infant says no, either verbally or perhaps by shaking his or her head. "No" is one of the infant's first and most important gestures. Is not the use of this gesture evidence of an existing sense of self that precedes making one's own the responses of the other, that is, that precedes the socialized object-self?

Against this position I would argue that the no is crucial for the development of the sense of self, not simply a manifestation of an already existing sense of self, and I would characterize the relationship between the use of no and the developing sense of self as a dialectical and mutually reinforcing one. For the self to have a sense of self it must consciously experience itself as bounded, as *not* the other, *not* the world, as a finite (quasi-) totality, albeit one whose boundary can be redefined. And, for this to occur, the self must experience itself not only as inhibited by the other—for example, when the infant is blocked from reaching a toy by an other or an object—but as conscious of its power to inhibit the other and, therefore, itself. The use of the verbal gesture no, or some variant thereof, is crucial in this process. Understanding the uniqueness of this gesture in the repertoire of verbal gestures learned by human beings provides a path for augmenting Mead's account of the self-as-object to allow for the development of a sense of self, a "self" that can eventually come to modify its own object-self. The term *self* in this chapter, unless specified otherwise, will be used when it is unnecessary to distinguish between the object-self and the sense of self.

A Concept of Limit

For there to be self, I presume that there must be that which is not-self. To say this is to say that there is a limit to the self, a boundary between self and other. Now this appears to be patently obvious, for if something is to be, it must in some way be demarcated from other things, and this is as true of the self as it is of anything else. However, the situation is immediately rendered more complex by the fact that it is usually presumed that if there is a self, there must be an awareness of this self—for example, as an object of consciousness in the case of the object-self, and as a consciousness that is aware of itself in the act of being aware of its possibilities in the case of the sense of self. The self is that which has both a limit and an awareness of that limit, an awareness of what it is not. But how helpful is this? After all, a dog would seem to have some sense that it is not a cat, or a house, and so on, yet we do not assume that a dog has a self. If having an awareness of one's limit is to be of assistance in demarcating the self, the awareness and/or the nature of the limit, the boundary, must differ qualitatively from the limit and/or the awareness of those creatures or organisms that we presume do not have selves.

The notion of limit, or boundary, will first have to be addressed in order to arrive at an explanation of how limits affect human consciousness and participate in the development of the self. Hegel's dialectic of limit, explicated in his *Science of Logic* and *Lesser Logic,* will be of help here. These works are meant to exhibit relationships between various concepts in a manner that will eventually lead the reader to recognize that seemingly independent (philosophical) concepts are in actuality aspects of an Absolute Idea. Here we are concerned not with Hegel's intentions in exhibiting relationships between various ideas, nor with providing an exhaustive commentary on his concept of limit, nor with whether his analysis of limit is applicable to every type or usage of the concept of limit, but only with how his analysis of limit can be of assistance in articulating the type of limit that is crucial for the development of the self.[1]

In the *Science of Logic* the first point Hegel wishes us to understand regarding the nature of limit is that we are dealing with a

1. For a more detailed discussion of the concept of limit, see my *Self-Winding Circle,* pp. 20–24.

qualitative, as opposed to a quantitative, concept. Were I to fence off a field, for example, and measure the size of the enclosure, I would have a quantitative limit, for the field would be measurable in quantitative terms. But what Hegel is interested in is qualitative limit, those qualities that make this thing not that thing—as, for example, in saying that this field is grassy but that one is sandy. Hegel is dealing with concepts, how they relate and how they differ from each other; thus, in his exposition he does not refer to what we might term material things, such as fields, but to concepts which at this stage of the *Science of Logic* are exceedingly abstract. In particular, he uses the terms "something" and "other" in the section of the *Logic* under consideration. Something must have a quality that makes it different from an other (something), and this quality must permeate, or be found throughout, the something. Because we are dealing with concepts containing virtually no prior determination, we are told that the determination of the something, that which makes it what it is as opposed to the other (something), is simply to *not be the other*. However, if the only determination of the something is to not be the other, then we are left with a rather paradoxical situation: something is only what it is, is only separate from the other, by itself being the non-being of the other. In other words, the non-being of the other is "contained" in the being of the something. The something's determination, which permeates its being, is to not be the other.

Something, as an immediate determinate being [*Dasein*], is, therefore, the limit relatively to another something, but the limit is present in the something itself, which is a something through the mediation of the limit which is just as much the non-being of the something. Limit is the mediation through which something and other each as well *is*, as *is not*.[2]

Something is what it is only because of its limit. The limit is the negation of the other, and this negation is not out there in the world, so to speak, but inhabits the something itself as its one and only determination. Something, however, "wishes" to "see" itself

---

2. Hegel, *Science of Logic*, p. 127; original emphasis. In the paragraphs that follow I shall use anthropomorphic terms such as *see, wish*, and *reject*, which are not part of Hegel's account of limit, but simply pedagogical devices of aid in expounding Hegel's dialectic.

as pure being surrounded by non-being, the non-being demarcating its limit. We find the something "rejecting" the non-being of the other, which it sees as invading its being, by declaring the limit outside itself. But the being of the something is defined only in terms of its non-being, its limit, which means that if this non-being were somehow placed outside of it, it would have no determination at all. It could not be a something.

The something is in contradiction with itself, for it is being as non-being. It is, and is not, its limit, and hence finds itself pressed by this contradiction into denial of its situation. Unreconciled to itself, it attempts to place non-being outside itself.[3] But it must fail in this attempt, because its determination is non-being. Hegel tells us that unreconciled contradiction is the essence of the finite, so that something that is, is forced into non-being by its very nature.

When we say of things that *they are finite,* we understand thereby that . . . non-being constitutes their nature and being. Finite things *are,* but their relation to themselves is that they are *negatively* self-related and in this very self-relation send themselves away beyond themselves, beyond their being. They *are,* but the truth of this being [*seins*] is their *end.*[4]

The finite something cannot escape from its determination as that which is imbued with non-being. Instead of overcoming this negativity through a dialectic that negates the negation itself, the negativity remains outer-directed, directed toward asserting what the something is in terms of what it *is not.* Finitude, for Hegel, can only be overcome by a negativity that negates from within, so to speak, as the negation of the negation.

In chapter 2 we looked at the relationship between Hegel's concept of temporality and Sartre's model of consciousness. Now we can see that Sartre's description of consciousness, as the nothing that nihilates in a perpetual flight from itself, resembles Hegel's description of the finite as that which has, and has not, its limit within. Consciousness is the perpetual nihilation that is directed

---

3. "Since the limit and the determinate being [*Dasein*] are each at the same time the negative of each other, the something, which *is* only in its limit, just as much separates itself from itself and points beyond itself to its non-being, declaring this to be its being and thus passing over into it" (*Science of Logic,* pp. 127–28; original emphasis).

4. Ibid., p. 129; original emphasis.

out of itself to what it is not, and as such is radically free and finite for Sartre. Hegel, on the other hand, would view this as the incessant unrest of the finite which unceasingly sees itself in terms of what it is not, without being conscious of its relationship to infinitude, without being aware of the dialectic of the negation of the negation.

However, what concerns us here is the concept of limit. For Sartre, as we have already seen, the sense of self is intimately connected with the (ideal) limit of pre-reflective consciousness, and entails the awareness of possibilities through being aware of what one lacks.[5] But to be aware of what one lacks is also to be aware of one's limit or limitations, so that the notion of limit is at the heart of the sense of self. However, even if one were to agree with certain basic elements of Sartre's description of the sense of self, one might still ask how the limit that eventually gives rise to the sense of self itself arises.

At first the self is abstract, undefined, and not yet self; it must have a boundary, something that sets it off from the other. How is an undefined being to achieve such a limit, one that will provide conscious differentiation from others, the world, the not-self? Perhaps we need look no further than the body, which is limited by its location in space and by its existence as a three-dimensional object with physical boundaries. But although bodily instantiation plays a role in the creation of boundaries—for example, when an infant is thwarted in its attempt to reach a bottle or breast—it cannot in itself explain the development of the boundary or boundaries necessary for a self.

The reason for this is not simply that there are many other "embodied" biological organisms seemingly without selves, but that the experience of having a body is itself mediated by our social experience. I come to view this body as my body, that is, as a body having certain characteristics, because I have viewed it from the perspective of the other and have internalized this perspective. In addition, Mead would make the following point: one's knowledge of bodily or physical things is, in general, related to the social nature of mind and the (object-) self. For Mead, knowledge of the physical thing is not due simply to vision. It incorporates tactile

5. See above, pp. 37–38, and 59–61.

experience, the experience of resistance (inertia), although one does not have to remain in contact with an object to possess knowledge of it. We can know the bodily characteristic of a thing at a distance, just as we can be aware of the inside of a physical thing that is being touched by the hand (even though its inside is at a distance from the hand). As a matter of fact, direct contact of this sort could never in itself supply us with knowledge of physical things. Mead tells us that to be bodily means to have an inside—which is at a distance from direct contact—as well as an outside, and that until objects are perceived of as having insides, they are not, properly speaking, known as physical things for human beings.

Were we to ask Mead how objects come to be perceived as having interiors, he would note the resistance that physical things offer us. Upon contact with an object, before it is known as a physical thing, I press against the object, and my experience is merely of pressing. The very young infant does not and cannot think about objects as having insides; they merely exist as focal points of effort. The question is then: How does an object come to have an inside which presses back, so to speak? This requires that the effort of which I am aware in the presence of the object be experienced as the object offering me resistance. Mead writes that "the organism in grasping and pushing things is identifying its own effort with the contact experience of the thing. . . . One arouses in himself an action which comes also from the inside of the thing."[6] One cannot know the physical thing as having an inside and an outside unless one can take both "roles"—that is, unless one can offer to oneself the resistance of the thing (as coming from inside the thing) and also respond to the resistance offered (by being outside the thing).

To be *conscious* of the inside of the object or to be aware of it as a physical thing, one must be able to evoke in himself the attitude of resisting; one must, prior to coming in contact with the distant object, seen or smelled, evoke in himself the "response" which the object will make to his grasping and handling it. This can be done only if a person is an object to himself, only, in *this* case, if one can respond to his own response (or action) as the other (the physical thing) does.[7]

6. *PP*, pp. 121–22.
7. Miller, *George Herbert Mead*, p. 64; original emphasis.

I do not wish to belabor this point here, nor to engage the metaphysical and epistemological questions raised by Mead's claims regarding the nature of physical objects. The point to be noted is that, for Mead, the notion of one's body as the basic source of the boundary for the (object-) self fails to account for how one comes to experience one's own body, or any physical thing, as bounded, as having an inside *and* an outside. Objects acting as focal points of effort cannot in themselves supply one with the capacity for being on the other side of the effort, outside oneself, in such a way that one experiences the resistance of an object as coming from an inside. And until one can experience objects as having outsides and insides, one will not be able to be consciously aware of one's body as having an interior whose boundary can be seen from the outside.

Kinaesthetic and visceral experiences can be located as inside our organisms only when these organisms have attained outsides. . . . [T]he child can delimit his bodily surfaces only through things not his body, and he reaches the entire surfaces of things not his body before he reaches his own organism as a bounded thing.[8]

In chapter 1 we saw how taking the response of the other and role-taking are basic to the development of the self as object. Here we have seen that for Mead even one's relationship to physical things is fundamentally altered through the capacity for making the response of the other one's own (in this case, of making the effort or resistance felt by oneself a property of the object as a physical thing with an inside). But just how does this capacity for being other (to self) lead to a self that is aware of its boundary and capable of altering it? If we rely solely on Mead's explanation of the developed self as an object of cognition, then the generalized other is responsible for the boundary of the (object-) self, and the wholeness of the (object-) self (of which one is aware) is but a reflection of the wholeness of the social order. Mead seeks to overcome the limitations of the self as a mere object of the generalized other by introducing the "I." However, for reasons discussed in the last chapter, this does not allow for the possibility of self-conscious control over what the self can become. The "I" is always outside

8. *PP,* p. 119.

the (object-) self, so that the self-as-object is always found as already delimited.

If there is to be self-determination, the self must be capable of undergoing change or modification—that is, the boundary or limit that sets the self apart from the not-self must be flexible—and the modifications must be accessible to some form of conscious control or direction. Following Hegel and his discussion of limit, I will argue that this boundary should be understood in terms of negation, and that the negative plays a decisive role in the development of the self-determining self. However, to arrive at the sense of self which allows for a form of self-determination, we must first look more closely at the role of negation and limit in the development of the object-self, which precedes and makes possible this sense of self.

Negation and the Object-Self

For Mead, the object-self is something that develops, and this development entails various stages and levels of sophistication in responding to the other and oneself. Before the child is able to conceptualize the roles he or she takes as roles, he or she "is aware of his response to the rôle, not of the rôle he is taking" (*MSS*, p. 372). Just why does the child take on responses of others which eventually take the shape of roles (which he or she becomes aware of as roles)? As a behaviorist, Mead places a great deal of weight on mechanisms of reinforcement. But Mead is not beyond bowing in Freud's direction when he claims that infants have biological impulses, and that the thwarting of these impulses through the introduction of taboos and prohibitions can lead to conflict within the organism.[9]

The prohibitions, the taboos, involve conflicting tendencies which appear in terms of personal commands. It is these that recur as imagery when the

9. Mead defines impulse in the following manner: "An impulse is a congenital tendency to react in a specific manner to a certain sort of stimulus, under certain organic conditions. Hunger and anger are illustrations of such impulses. They are best termed 'impulses,' and not 'instincts,' because they are subject to extensive modifications in the life-history of individuals, and these modifications are so much more extensive than those to which the instincts of lower animal forms are subject that the use of the term 'instinct' in describing the behavior of normal adult human individuals is seriously inexact" (*MSS*, p. 337). For further clarification and discussion of the terms *impulse* and *instinct,* see below, ch. 5.

impulse again arises to do the forbidden thing. Where an animal would only slink back from a forbidden spot, the child repeats the prohibition in the rôle of the parent. . . . What was part of an unbroken flow becomes now an event which precedes breaking of the law or compliance with it. [MSS, p. 375]

The taking of the response of the other, the no, the prohibition, gathers within the child both impulse and prohibition. The child desires something, but "in the rôle of the parent the object is taboo. . . . The child's capacity for being the other puts both of these characters of the object before him in their disparateness" (p. 375). In Freudian terms, the infant has identified with the other so as to internalize the other as the aspect of the psyche known as the superego.[10] While Mead is well aware that conflict is generated by the introduction of prohibitions in the form of the parental no, he is not as interested in exploring the emotional repercussions of this intrusion as he is in showing how conflict of this sort fosters new ways of shaping and adjusting to the environment.

In a word, the sympathetic assumption of the attitude of the other brings into play varying impulses which direct the attention to features of the object which are ignored in the attitude of direct response. And the very diverse attitudes assumed furnish the material for a reconstruction of the objective field in which and through which the co-operative social act may take place, giving satisfactory expression to all the rôles involved. It is this analysis and reconstruction which is rendered possible by the apparatus of the vocal gesture, with its related organic equipment. [pp. 375–76]

At this point, Mead proceeds to minimize the psychological repercussions of the conflict by introducing temporal disjunction. One does not feel the impulse and prohibition at the same moment, which could easily yield a state of inner turmoil, but one has the advantage of seeing the various sides of the conflict from the perspective of responses or roles that are separated temporally. Following the last line of the above passage, Mead states:

10. "A considerable amount of aggressiveness must be developed in the child against the authority which prevents him from having his first, but none the less his most important, satisfactions. . . . By means of identification he takes the unattackable authority into himself. The authority now turns into his super-ego" (Sigmund Freud, *Civilization and Its Discontents,* p. 76; all references to this book are to Norton's pagination).

It is in this field that the continuous flow breaks up in ordered series, in the relation of alternative steps leading up to some event. Time with its distinguishable moments enters, so to speak, with intervals necessary to shift the scene and change the costumes. One cannot be another and yet himself except from the standpoint of a time which is composed of entirely independent elements. [p. 376]

The immediate, or specious, present is to be contrasted with the extended present of thought or reflection. The extended present is mediated by problems and doubts and makes reference to a past and a future.[11] When faced with problems, one is moved to reflect; in reflecting, one nurtures an object-self and experiences "time with its distinguishable moments." For Mead, the development of the object-self is closely connected with temporality, as the above passages show. One cannot occur without the other. What Mead does not appear sufficiently sensitive to is the degree to which the characteristics of consciousness and conflict play havoc with the experiential independence of past, present, and future for the young child in the context under consideration. Even if we analyze the experience of temporality for the consciousness which has a developed object-self, that is, adult consciousness, we discover—as William James pointed out long ago in his *Principles of Psychology*—that consciousness contains a fringe, or halo, effect, and we must be most careful in speaking of independent moments.[12] Are we not safe in assuming that a young child, who does not have a fully developed object-self and a reflective consciousness, and who does not live in the knife-edge present of the abstract sciences but pri-

11. "Only when habits or impulsive behavior are frustrated do we become conscious and reconstruct behavior. . . . But [self-] consciousness means reference to something not present, not in the specious passing present. It at once involves a past and a future, and both the past and the future referred to are hypothetical" (Miller, *George Herbert Mead*, p. 39).

12. William James, "The Stream of Thought," pp. 67–69. It is worth noting that Mead describes the experience of passing events as follows: "Our specious present as such is very short. We do, however, experience passing events; part of the process of the passage of events is directly there in our experience, including some of the past and some of the future. We see a ball falling as it passes, and as it does pass part of the ball is covered and part is being uncovered. We remember where the ball was a moment ago and we anticipate where it will be beyond what is given in our experience" (*MSS*, p. 176).

marily in the realm of the immediate, experiences the taking of the prohibitions of the other and the original prohibited impulse as happening simultaneously? The introduction of the negative sets the organism at odds with itself, so that it feels conflicted. The organism is in contradiction with itself, and this does not happen because at one moment the organism feels the prohibition and at another the impulse, but because the feelings exist simultaneously.

At this point, it will be useful to return to Hegel, who claims that true thought, reason, grasps the reality of contradiction, while a less complete mode of thought, the understanding (*Verstand*), seeks to avoid contradiction by separating contradictory elements. One pole of the contradiction is placed in this time or space frame, the other in another time or space frame. Whether Hegel is right regarding contradiction in general is not at issue. The point is that Mead does seem to have fallen prey to the understanding, to borrow Hegel's language, in the passages quoted above by avoiding the reality and importance of *felt* contradiction. Conflict arises within an impulsive organism that can internalize prohibitions. Mead avoids the psychological import of this experience by moving too quickly to a level at which contradiction is resolved by separating roles (or impulses and prohibitions) into different time frames.

The burgeoning conflicted consciousness is what it is by being itself and not being itself, that is, being other to itself. This tension can be resolved, but while it lasts, we have a variant of what Mead calls sociality, the being between of the given (impulse) and the new (prohibition). In the case of the infant, we do not as yet have a consciousness aware of its sociality, but we have a consciousness which has experienced the not-self, the other, appearing in its midst.

In sum, the taking of the response of the parental figure in the form of a prohibition, or limit, introduces negativity into consciousness. Once this negativity has been introduced, the child experiences a form of otherness, though not yet the otherness of the other as a series of discrete responses, or roles.[13] This otherness takes the form of feeling that one is and is not one's desire, of feeling the no while feeling the desire, or impulse. This situation occurs

13. The term *child* is used to denote an individual in that stretch of life which begins in what is usually termed infancy and runs through the first few years.

before the cognitive self-as-object fully develops, and before the Sartrean sense of self arises. The former is not yet fully present, because it requires the integration of complex sets of responses, which, in turn, necessitates the resolution of conflicting impulses and prohibitions. (In some fashion the burgeoning object-self must make its peace with the prohibitions of the other in order to have a systemic "me" unriddled by contradiction.) The latter is not yet present, because the sense of self, while depending on the presence of the negative in consciousness, requires a negative that has passed through the development of a reflective stage. It is only after one has learned how to take the role of the other and has integrated complex responses and roles, that there is an indentifiable object-self to which pre-reflective consciousness can relate in its flight toward what it is not, what it lacks. The pre-reflective sense of self is the non-cognitively lived consciousness that has learned to live in sociality, between what it has been and the non-being of the future.

But we have moved too quickly here in discussing reflection and the sense of self, for we have not yet fully addressed the mechanisms for internalizing the no, and how the no functions as a limit in the development of the object-self. Here, Freud can help us. Originally, Freud tells us, the infant experiences a boundless narcissism; the other makes no demands, and the reality principle is as yet undeveloped. In this state, which can be referred to as primary narcissism, the infant is immersed in an oceanic feeling of oneness—both the ego and the superego are absent.[14] This feeling, of course, cannot last, for such basic needs as the need for food call for a dependence on something (for example, the mother's breast or the bottle) that is not always immediately available.

According to Freud, inner and outer come to be distinguished in terms of the locus of sensations, that is, the immediate presence of sensations derived from within the child's own body versus those of sensations derived in conjunction with external sources, for example, pain from touching a hot stove. While I would want to avoid the terms "inner" and "outer" to describe this state, espe-

---

14. "An infant at the breast does not as yet distinguish his ego from the external world as the source of the sensations flowing in upon him. He gradually learns to do so, in response to various promptings." (Freud, *Civilization and its Discontents*, pp. 13–14).

cially given the rather primitive experiences that Freud is describing, the point worthy of note here is that the total non-differentiation of self and world soon gives way to some degree of awareness of otherness. Eventually we find that the world has impinged to such an extent that the adult's "ego-feeling is . . . only a shrunken residue of a much more inclusive—indeed, an all-embracing—feeling which corresponded to a more intimate bond between the ego and the world about it." [15]

The dissolution of the state of boundlessness rapidly escalates when the infant moves from the stage of experiencing merely alien sensations and begins to encounter prohibitions, not only as external barriers that prevent the satisfaction of desires—for example, in the denial of the mother's breast or the bottle—but as the internal voice of the developing superego. In discussing Mead's remarks on the introduction of taboos, I commented that, while he is aware of their importance in creating conflict for the child, he does not seem to fully appreciate the unique importance of the negative in giving rise to the trauma of psychic contradiction. Freud is of assistance here precisely because he is sensitive to just how crucial the no is in splitting the psyche through the development of the superego, and in seeing how this fundamentally alters the relationship of the organism to itself. The superego, which is comparable to, though not identical with, Mead's generalized other, serves a multitude of functions for Freud. He states:

On previous occasions we have been driven to the hypothesis that some such agency develops in our ego which may cut itself off from the rest of the ego and come into conflict with it. We have called it the 'ego ideal,' and by way of functions we have ascribed to it self-observation, the moral conscience, the censorship of dreams, and the chief influence in repression. [16]

Freud later came to call the ego ideal the superego, and he traced its development to various mechanisms; for example, the Oedipus complex is thought to play an important role in its genesis. [17] I am

15. Ibid., p. 15.

16. Freud, *Group Psychology and the Analysis of the Ego,* pp. 41–42 in Norton's pagination.

17. "Conscience develops through the family relationships of the oedipus complex and the way these are eventually given up in becoming and transforming the

not interested here in the oedipal dimensions of the development of the superego, but in features of its development that can be said to pre-date the oedipal phase.

The development of the ego consists in a departure from the primary narcissism and results in a vigorous attempt to recover it. This departure is brought about by means of the displacement of libido to an ego-ideal imposed from without, while gratification is derived from the attainment of this ideal.[18]

The organism, which had begun to develop a reality principle in terms of the absence or presence of sensations, now has to deal with being split, so to speak, from within. The voice of the other appears to say no at the same time that the desire is present for which the prohibition is intended. The child has a special need for learning the verbal gesture no. No-saying to the other is crucial if the child is to come to terms with the entrance of the negative into consciousness. The child doesn't simply repeat the word *no* to the other, he or she identifies with the no-saying parental figure in order to lessen the tension felt in containing both the no and the prohibited impulse; the prohibitions are converted into the ego ideal. "To this ideal ego [superego] is now directed the self-love which the real ego enjoyed in childhood. The narcissism seems to be now displaced on to this new ideal ego, which, like the infantile ego, deems itself the possessor of all perfections."[19]

This statement refers to the culmination of the process in the adult, but I want to emphasize that this process of identifying with the voice of the "oppressor," the parent, begins very early in life. The power of the parent is overwhelming. Survival depends on identifying with this power, using it, harnessing it, making oneself over in its image. For the child to overcome the fear of the other

---

superego itself. The ego ideal develops throughout life, through identifications later with people and/or ideas as well as with parents in childhood. Freud does not explain how the superego as observer arises. It arises, presumably, beginning with the first experience of self as different from the other—of self as object as well as subject" (Nancy Chodorow, *The Reproduction of Mothering: Psychoanalysis and the Sociology of Gender*, p. 44n).

18. Freud, "On Narcissism: An Introduction," p. 57.

19. Ibid., p. 51.

and the perpetual frustration of conflict, the child must in some sense become the other.[20]

By means of identification he takes the unattackable authority into himself. The authority now turns into his super-ego and enters into possession of all the aggressiveness which a child would have liked to exercise against it. . . . The relationship between the super-ego and the ego is a return, distorted by a wish, of the real relationships between the ego, as yet undivided, and an external object.[21]

We can see here an impetus other than (and in addition to) the parents' reinforcement of the child's behavior for why the child takes the response of the other and makes it his or her own. In the case of the verbal gesture no, the young child takes (over) the response of the other in order to protect him or her self from a state of internal conflict. The child says no as the parent does, and the focus of the no is his or her own prohibited impulse. The child comes to respond as the other has responded, and the otherness of the response is neutralized in the process. The no comes to be experienced as (object-) self in opposition to impulse. The interpenetration in consciousness of impulse opposing prohibition is resolved when the no is thought of as an aspect of the (burgeoning) object-self—the impulse being rendered as not-self for this consciousness.

But this cannot be the whole story, the whole self, for negativity has fundamentally altered the nature of consciousness. We may recall here Hegel's claim that a qualitative limit is the non-being of the other, but a non-being of the other that must be in the something itself. The non-being of the other is not an external boundary but a limit that resides within. Psychologically speaking, one's limit must be internal, a property, or object, of one's consciousness. If it were not within, it would not, by definition, be a *psycho*logical limit. Such a limit cannot be out there in the world but must exist in some form as a self-limit of which one can be, or is, aware, as a form of qualitative limit.

Once the conflict between the no and the impulse has arisen, the

20. Freud declares that the child can tolerate ambivalent feelings that the adult cannot (see, for example, Freud's comments in *A General Introduction to Psychoanalysis,* pp. 341–42). Nevertheless, it is also true that he is well aware that there are situations that call for and require the resolution of conflict for the child.

21. Freud, *Civilization and its Discontents,* p. 76.

child can make use of two strategies for dealing with the dissonance. In one, the child comes to identify with the prohibition and transforms the no of the other into his or her own, as we have already seen. In another, the organism resists the no of the other and remains with the impulse, as if to eject the no from consciousness. In this resistance, though, the child is caught in a paradox analogous to the "something" in Hegel's dialectic of limit. In Hegel's dialectic, the non-being of the other becomes the something's being, and something finds itself in contradiction to itself. The something then attempts to eject from itself the non-being through which it has come to be defined. Non-being must be placed outside the something if the something is to maintain its integrity—its limit must be outside itself. We—the observers of the process—know, however, that non-being remains the definition of the something. The no that the something says to non-being is itself a manifestation of the negativity with which it is permeated. It can only say no because non-being resides within it, so that in the attempt to refuse non-being, the something contradicts itself.

In the case of the burgeoning object-self, the negative of the other has insinuated its way into consciousness through the earliest experiences of prohibition. But, as we have seen, once the organism has both the no and the impulse for which the response of no is called out, an internal conflict arises, which we can now refer to—albeit somewhat metaphorically—as a contradiction entailing being and non-being. The being (impulse) of the child wishes to deny non-being (the no), but non-being has already become part of its being, its consciousness. One resolution of the conflict takes the form of continuing to seek to deny entrance to the no by ejecting it from consciousness, as the "something" seeks to eject non-being from its midst. We know, however, that non-being is already present in the child's consciousness, for the process of denial requires negation. The other resolution to the conflict entails identification with the prohibitions in the development of the superego, and this alternative will have to be followed (to some degree) if the child is not to remain at an infantile stage of continual no-saying. This course of action will have the further advantage of allowing the individual to come to terms eventually not only with societal prohibitions, but with his or her existence as a being for whom non-being has a unique significance.

Before proceeding to examine how the development of the object-self, dependent as it is on negativity, relates to the rise of the sense of self, we should place several of the claims made regarding the object-self in the context of Sartre's account of the look. In Sartre's description of the look, the selfness that is looked-at is on the level of pre-reflective consciousness and at first is not aware of itself as an object. The meeting of consciousness with (another) consciousness calls for a limit that can separate and hold apart one from the other. And because consciousness can only be limited by consciousness, this takes place, we are informed, in the acceptance of the me-as-object that the other produces by looking at me.

But this limit can neither come from me nor be thought by me, for I can not limit myself; otherwise I should be a finite totality. On the other hand, in Spinoza's terms, thought can be limited only by thought. Consciousness can be limited only by my consciousness. Now we can grasp the nature of my Self as-object: it is the limit between two consciousnesses as it is pro-duced by the limiting consciousness and assumed by the limited conscious-ness.[BN, p. 286]

This limit is neither for-itself nor in-itself; rather, it is a being-for-others, "divided between two negations with opposed origins and opposite meanings" (p. 286). We have, and have not, this limit, because it arises and exists only in and through our relationships with others.

Sartre also argues that I can maintain the integrity of my con-sciousness only by refusing to be the me-as-object. I must negate the object-me that the other creates and refuses. "I escape the Other by leaving him with my alienated Me in his hands" (p. 285). How-ever, I cannot completely deny the object-me because: (1) it is me in the form of an object; (2) I can only protect myself and separate from the other if there is a limit or barrier present through which I maintain myself as a spontaneous consciousness. The refused me-as-object serves as this barrier. By accepting it as my refused me, I rob the other of the opportunity to use it in order to make me into an object. I then proceed to turn the other into an object. This task is not a difficult one, for the other has become the one who exists only in refusing to be me, and this refusal to be me is now an object of my consciousness.

Sartre would agree with the account of object-self and limit presented so far to the extent that limit can exist only if there is being-for-others. But he would not agree in seeing negation as internalized from the other, because for him, it is consciousness itself that is nothing and that gives rise to nihilations. The power of the other is acknowledged in terms of the look, which provides the me-as-object.

This me-as-object is analogous to the object-self of Mead—in that it is the other which gives rise to the self-as-object—although Sartre discusses the me-as-object on the level of pre-reflective consciousness, while Mead assumes that the object-self exists on the reflective level (although it does arise from a non-reflective state, that is, a non-self-conscious state).[22] For Mead, the object-self does not fundamentally develop in hostility to the other, as it does for Sartre, but out of reinforced responses and role-taking. Mead's account of the genesis of the object-self is much more thorough than Sartre's description of the me-as-object, whereas Sartre's account points to the importance of conflict in a way that Mead's does not. Mead sees conflict engendered by the no of the other primarily in terms of the ongoing development of rationality and mastery of the social world.

In the model I have been developing, I have attempted to compensate for Mead's lack of sensitivity to the impact of conflict (that is, to the *felt* contradiction it gives rise to) by addressing the importance of the negative as prohibition. For, to my way of thinking, the internalization of prohibitions is of exceptional importance in the genesis of the object-self and, as I shall try to show in the next section, for the sense of self. Negation is introduced from outside the body of the organism, but it is rapidly transformed into a primary constituent of the (self-) conscious mind. Limit is viewed in this model as a form of qualitative negation, in the sense that the experience of being told no, of thinking no, permeates the consciousness of the one who is aware of it. It is the pervasive quality of this no in conjunction with impulse that gives rise to tension and dissonance within the organism. Dissonance calls for resolution, and the resolution requires one to make use of negation, by either accepting it as part of oneself or using the negative to reject the no

22. Of course, Sartre also discusses an object-self on the reflective level as a quasi-object in impure reflection, as we saw in ch. 2.

of the other. The mechanisms for dealing with prohibitions further the importance and the power of the negative from which the organism is attempting to flee.

Sartre, then, is not entirely incorrect in speaking of (self-) consciousness as nothing; as an awareness that has become aware of itself, it has struggled with and internalized negation almost from the start. The confrontation with negation normally promotes the process of becoming an object-self, for example, by acting as a stimulus to take the role of the parent in order to overcome dissonance. Also, the no as a verbal gesture assists the child in rejecting certain prohibitions of the other, which, in turn, promotes demarcation from the other. (Note the seemingly obsessive use of the word no by the two-year old who is demarcating object-self from other.) The object-self develops not only by taking the responses of others, including prohibitions, but also by practicing, as it were, how not to accept specific demands of others, through use of the verbal gesture no. It appears that Spinoza's insight that all determination is negation is not far from the mark where (self-) consciousness is involved.

From very early on, the human being is presented with the alternative of either rejecting or identifying with the other, to put it in its simplest terms. Clearly, this process is not thought through by the infant or young child. The child responds, and in responding becomes habituated to "choosing" among alternatives before the choices are consciously determined. Eventually, in responding from the role of the other, the child comes to have a consciousness of object-self and alternatives to object-self; it is only by taking the role of the other that he or she develops an appreciation for the existence of alternatives. But for an individual to become self-determining, there must first be an object-self that one consciously identifies as me, and then a sense of self in which one's own possibilities appear as not-me. We now turn to how the elements involved in the process of developing the object-self give rise to the sense of self.

The Sense of Self

The major elements entailed in the genesis of the sense of self have already been alluded to in the previous sections of this chapter. What remains to be accomplished is the articulation and integration of these elements so as to exhibit how a sense of self arises, and how it provides for the possibility of self-determination. I should note in advance that while the sense of self is dependent on its social context for its development, and while certain social environments are more conducive than others to its growth and sustenance, I leave the exploration of these topics to the next chapter. Here I address the features of the self's development that lead to the sense of self by beginning with a summary of the object-self's development.

Immediate gratification of impulses gives way to the inhibition of impulses as the young child develops. I say *inhibition* because I refer not simply to the failure to have an impulse satisfied, as when an infant is hungry and the parent(s) cannot respond immediately, but to the internalization of the prohibitions. Prohibitions arise in the form of the no. In turn, the use of the no by the child takes the form of a verbal gesture, or perhaps at an earlier stage the form of a shaking of the head. By acquiring the ability to make the verbal gesture, the child can say no to that which is insisting on prohibitions. At first, however, the other (the parent) is needed, is powerful, and must be obeyed. Conflict is generated between impulse and prohibition, which gives rise to identification with the no of the other, so that the prohibition is internalized. The child says no to him or her self as the parent would; the child takes the behavior, and eventually the role of, the other, and is reinforced for so doing. Of course, the child is also reinforced for taking on other behaviors, but it is the negative that is especially significant for understanding self-consciousness and self-determination. The negative, by producing tension, fosters the identification with the other(s); this identification is crucial to the development of the object-self and also allows for the eventual development of the sense of self. The object-self, then, arises as the child takes on complex behaviors and roles, which in turn allow the child to reflect, that is, to see him or her self from the perspective of the other. This object-self attains its most complete development when the other becomes sufficiently abstract to allow the self to be an object of the generalized other. Mead argues that object-selves are never identical, because each mirrors the whole in a unique fashion, and, in this respect, we are Leibnizian monads of the social world.[23]

As the object-self develops, the child makes use of the no in order

23. See ch. 1 above.

to assist in satisfying impulses—which differ in intensity from individual to individual—by rejecting the no of the other. The child also employs the no to renounce what is viewed as not object-self once the object-self has begun to form and comes to learn to say no to its own impulses (as the original impulses are denied in favor of the developing object-self). Given these factors, the no-saying of any two individuals will never be identical, and differentiation from the other(s) tends to accelerate as the capacity for no-saying becomes further developed.

The self is not merely an object-self, as Mead would hold. In the development of the sense of self (which, as I shall show, includes but supersedes the object-self), novelty plays a crucial role. An infant is neither very knowledgeable nor very experienced in the ways of the world, and the unexpected often happens just as he or she is learning what to expect. Quite aside from the metaphysical question regarding the status of novelty in the universe, the responses of parents and adults, due to their complexity alone, will often appear to the young child as unexpected events. Expert and lay advice commonly given to parents of a newborn is to be consistent in responding to their infant; consistency is highly valued in a world that can easily fragment because it has not yet had time to solidify. But it is not only the responses of the external world that are apt to appear unexpected; children are often startled by their own responses once they have come to expect certain patterns of behavior. Hence, in learning what to expect from others and him or her self, the child learns to expect the unexpected. (Do we not exhibit an intuitive awareness of the necessity of the infant coming to terms with the novel when, even in the earliest days of their lives, we play games such as peek-a-boo?)

In Mead's language, the "I" often responds in novel ways, which the burgeoning object-self as "me" comes to accommodate. Early in the development of the object-self, the child begins to learn that he or she must live in sociality, the betwixt-and-between that occurs as a system adapts to the introduction of the new. The organism must become habituated to both being itself and not being itself, to being both object-self and other, if the organism is to adapt itself to the human condition. The consciousness of limit, the awareness of the (internal) non-being of oneself that is required for a fully realized sense of self, develops in part from the repeated challenge to the organism to integrate what it does not expect to be part of itself with itself.

First there is impulse, then prohibition. Use of the verbal gesture no and identification with prohibitions give rise to a being that contains negation. Role-taking develops the object-self but develops it at the same time that the capacity for saying no to the other and to one's own impulses is also developing. Novelty forces the evolving object-self into transition, and thus one becomes habituated to living in-between, to living in sociality, that is, between the object-self and that which one is not. Non-being, limit, has insinuated itself into consciousness, so that consciousness comes to experience itself as that which lacks, and can experience this lack, as we shall see, even when it is not reflecting.

Sartre holds the position that reflective consciousness is derived from the pre-reflective, in that the pre-reflective attempts to gain a unity (which it cannot have) through reflection. However, as I see it, the pre-reflective sense of self comes into being only after the object-self and the not-self have arisen, and it depends on reflection in order to develop. It is only by becoming other to oneself through social interaction that one can become aware of (object-) self and other(ness), and until one has this awareness, it is not possible to speak of the lack that comes to inhabit pre-reflective consciousness (unless one wants to presume a magical nothingness as the definition of consciousness). If there is a preceding unity that pre-reflective or reflective consciousnes is tempted to wax nostalgic about under certain circumstances, it is of a non-reflective state prior to the introduction of the other through prohibitions and roles.

In the development of the self, consciousness becomes used to, habituated to, the world of the not-self, and this not-self becomes present to consciousness through prohibitions and in learning to expect the unexpected. One begins to live in a world of anticipation—that is, a world of the coming to be that is not and might not be—and the future is approached as that which is not-self and as holding open the possibility of novelty. Sociality and the internalization of the negative together produce a consciousness which, even when it does not explicitly reflect on itself, that is, make of itself an object, orients itself in the world by moving toward that which it is not, and this is evident in the roles we take and live.

Take Sartre's example of the waiter who is, and is not, a waiter. Sartre claims that this being and non-being follow from the very nature of pre-reflective consciousness as nothing, which at each moment separates itself from itself through nothing, and which can lead to the deeper separation of reflection. It is actually more accurate to say that the waiter is, and is not, a waiter on the pre-reflective level, because he or she has come to have a consciousness that can refer to itself through the limits that encompass it as a waiter. If, on the pre-reflective level, a waiter is so thoroughly immersed in what he or she is doing that there is no awareness of the activity of waitering either through anticipating the behavior of others (for example, that of the customer) or through being aware of what one has yet to do, that is, of what is lacking (in not setting the table, in not serving the fish), then there is only the behavior of a waiter, and not the pre-reflective consciousness of a waiter. Here I have extended the notion of lack from what the object-self lacks to what there is to be done in a specific role or activity, but this is a legitimate extension because it is my pre-reflective self that is related to and must do what has to be done, and the doing of it negates the lack in the world that is directly dependent on myself.[24] The pre-reflective has a teleological dimension because it non-reflectively anticipates events, events "haunted" by their non-being, and because it is aware of that which it lacks.

Experiences of immersion, in which there is neither a pre-reflective sense of self nor a reflective object-self, are very unlikely to occur in the context of interacting with others. Interaction calls on us to anticipate, and anticipation entails both the expected response and the possibility of an unexpected response by the other. In the presence of the other, one is often forced to come to terms with the unexpected and one learns to live with the not-self that

24. On the pre-reflective level I move through the world negating that which is not-self in order to identify it as related to or encompassed by my consciousness. Negation is present as qualitative limit within, but that which is not-self is open to negativity being turned on it in order to negate it as not-self and make it self, so that it can be said: one modifies the self by working on the world. The negativity that consciousness wields transforms the not-self into the self by negating, dare I say it, the negation (that is, the not-self), and thereby alters the qualitative limit of the self. See ch. 5 below for further discussion and clarification of the relation between negativity and work.

appears as the new. We are much more likely to lose ourselves in situations that reduce and keep to a minimum novel stimuli or, better still, situations in which we do not expect to meet the unexpected. I have in mind, for example, the singing of repetitive chants in quiet surroundings, which can produce trance-like states. If one is isolated from others and engaged in familiar activities, this too may give rise to the experience of losing oneself—for example, when driving late at night down an uncrowded road that one has driven down many times before. (In the latter case, we see the danger of not having an anticipatory consciousness. It should be noted, however, that what is often described as losing oneself is not a loss of the sense of self, but rather, a loss of the object-self.) Of course, none of these circumstances necessarily give rise to immersion, because the generalized other and the realm of the not-self serve as companions, as it were, for those who have developed language, internalized prohibitions, and lived in sociality.

Before proceeding, clarification is in order regarding the terms *not-self* and *anticipation*. There are three distinct, but interrelated, usages of *not-self* in the present discussion. The first meaning is quite broad: the not-self is all that the self is not now nor has been; it is what it can be only in the future. The awareness of this very general not-self arises in part because of the unexpected, the novel. A more restricted meaning of the term is simply the new or novel when referred to in connection with the self. Finally, the term refers to what one specifically is not, that is, what one lacks—and, of course, one always lacks the novel on first encounter.

The term *anticipation* involves the specificity found in the latter usage of *not-self*, for that which one anticipates is an event or particular that "is not yet." But it also avails itself of the broader connotation of not-self, for, by definition, what "is not yet" is of the future, and is not [accessible to (self-) consciousness]. In anticipation consciousness is aware of its limit, that is, the limit of its awareness as a pre-reflective consciousness. And, though it is "personal," it need not be seen as having selfness because the non-being or absence is perceived of as "out there" in the world, rather than from "within" (so as to be "my" lack). However, since the anticipated provides a "my-ness" to consciousness in the form of a limit to awareness, and since it does this through an awareness of the non-being or absence of what is yet to be, it will be treated here as giving rise to a sense of self, though the intensity of the latter is not as great as that deriving from the awareness of lack. When it comes to the question of self-determination, in fact, it is the not-self as lack that proves to be most crucial.

One does not have to reflect on the object-self to experience its presence, for it is the *here* from which consciousness steps out into the world; yet, at any moment, aspects of it may be brought before or to consciousness as consciousness reflects on itself. The not-self does not have to be reflected on at every moment to be experienced; it is the *there* into which consciousness sets forth. Both can be reflected on and were originally experienced as objects of reflection as the object-self developed.

Human beings are not simply object-selves. By living in sociality, human beings become conscious of what they are not, in the manner discussed above. This gives rise to a consciousness that is aware of the not-self, as part of its pre-reflective experience. This awareness is not due to an I behind consciousness, but to consciousness mediating self and not-self. Sartre claims that we have an indirect awareness of self on the pre-reflective level. I wish to argue that this awareness is to be understood in terms of the present of consciousness acting as a sort of fulcrum between the anticipated—as the not yet available—or the not-self as lack, and the immediate past of consciousness. In this pre-reflective awareness, the object-self is (indirectly) referred to in anticipation, for where one locates the not-self as (ideal) limit refers back to what and where one has been as an object-self. Anticipations and absences (which are experienced with varying degrees of interest and intensity) give rise to a consciousness that is not merged with a single object, one that therefore has an awareness that overreaches the immediate; this awareness translates into consciousness's presence to itself as an indirect awareness of "self." One can also move to the reflective level and bring the object-self under the gaze of consciousness through reflecting on what has been. However, the reflection on the object-self that exists on the reflective level of consciousness is now no longer the (simple) reflection on roles or behaviors that Mead discusses, that is found in childhood. Consciousness has become habituated to living in sociality on the pre-reflective level, and as such it is sensitive to riding between (object-) self and not-self, even when there is no direct reflection on the object-self. It lives in a world in which one must regularly greet the unexpected and experience the presence of the not-self. The lack of pre-reflective consciousness sensitizes and informs reflective consciousness, making the reflective consciousness of the adult quite different from that of the child. Not only is the object of consciousness more complex, but so is the awareness of what one is not. Informed ignorance nurtures the self.

The child experiences both an evolving object-self and a non-reflective consciousness that has yet to develop a sense of self. It is no accident that the child refers to himself or herself in the third person, as a name among other names, before he or she can experience Sartre's sense of self. The adult has learned to live in between (object-) self and not-self on the level of pre-reflective consciousness, aware that an object-self is indirectly present due to the openness of consciousness to the not-self. The lack experienced by consciousness relates consciousness to its own past—both the past of the cognitively accessible object-self and the immediate past of what has just gone before consciousness—so that consciousness has the pre-reflective experience of being and non-being. Reflection tends to promote a dualism of subject and object, whereas the pre-reflective consciousness of the sense of self lives the quasi-unity of a stream of consciousness open to the future. The present of consciousness, to use Sartre's expression, is a detotalized totality: it is a (quasi-) totality because it relates object-self and not-self by being the limit of both, the non-being of each that relates each to the other; it is detotalized because it is open to the not-self, to what it lacks.

Must a transcendental ego be posited here as the source of unity that integrates the not-self into a new object-self? No such "third man" need be posited. In the development of the object-self, the novel is integrated into the old me-system, while the system reorganizes itself, so to speak, due to the presence of the novel element. The ecosystem into which a mutation is introduced either accommodates itself to the mutation by altering itself, or the mutation appears as too different from the given system to allow it to be incorporated. In an analogous fashion, the novel element that is to be integrated into an existing me-system must not be absolutely novel or it will not be able to insinuate its way into the existing system. Systems undergo alteration due to the characteristics of the system *and* the novel event, so that one does not have to posit an ego that integrates the system above and beyond the relationships within the system. The object-self is a relational and open system, which is altered by the novel in the integration of the novel.

Self-determination cannot be understood in terms of free will. And, though reflection is crucial to self-determination, for both the initial development of the object-self and its realization, self-determination cannot be understood solely as the result of cognition (reflection) in the manner that Mead seems to suggest. Self-determination is the capacity to adjust a limit of the self by negating the not-self, so as to convert that which is other or imperfectly self into self, and it depends on the internalization of the no. One is not simply a thing, an in-itself, but an open system living in sociality. The individual is not determined to be or to act in a certain manner, as a result of having some kind of a fixed soul or self, because sociality requires and allows frequent alteration of the self. Having experienced the pre-reflective consciousness that has the not-self as lack within it, the individual comes to expect that he or she does not have a fixed relationship to the world, and negation of the not-self confirms this by reshaping the world for the individual. On the one hand, one can only be self-determined in the context of what one has been, and it would be an act of ignorance or bad faith to deny the facticity of the object-self. On the other hand, once one becomes aware of one's relationship to the other, to the novel, to living in sociality, as well as of the power of the negative (which one has internalized and which resides in consciousness), one can act to negate aspects of the not-self, and in altering them, thereby alter the horizon of one's self.

To be aware of a limit opens up the possibility of moving beyond the limit by giving oneself a new limit. As the individual matures and becomes more aware of that which is object-self in contrast to not-self, the reflective organizing of the object-self by consciousness becomes possible. In an ecosystem, the system either can or cannot tolerate the introduction of novelty, for natural selection holds sway. But once a creature emerges that is aware of its sociality, it can reflect on that which does not, or will not, mesh with an old me-system, and it can become aware of internal contradictions in the me-system. The me-system is complex, and certain elements may be more conducive to its functioning and development than others; reflection on the me-system leads to the possibility of augmenting the object-self through what once appeared as not-self but now comes to be seen as capable of integration through new knowledge and experience. The capacity for self-determination emerges in the context of sociality, entails the internalization of the no, and comes to fruition when I am sufficiently aware of the object-self and not-self to be able to say that this possible integration of the me and not-me is the me to come; it is the lack I experience now that must, and can, be overcome. The "trick," then, in becoming a self-determining self is to use the sensitivities acquired in the development of the sense of self to allow for alterations of the self not only on the pre-reflective level (that is, when one responds to the lack without reflecting), but on the level of reflective consciousness as well.

I have been speaking as if, once the development of the self is set in motion, the natural outcome is a self that is capable of self-determination. Yet such a self, entailing both the object-self and the sense of self, does not develop in isolation, and its relationships to society and to others act to inhibit or stimulate its development. In the next chapter, then, we will look at a key feature of the self's relation to others, the dialectic of recognition, and will further articulate just how an individual is to be seen as self-determining.

CHAPTER FIVE

The Circumscribed Self

Domination and Self-Determination

Introduction

IN DISCUSSING THE DEVELOPMENT OF THE SENSE OF SELF AND its relationship to self-determination, I have stressed the importance of the internalization of the negative, and the manner in which the self's development is linked to sociality.[1] But to understand the move from the potential for self-determination to its realization, the discussion must be enlarged to include specific sorts of social relationships, if only to acknowledge that societies devise different prohibitions, and that the intensity and nature of these prohibitions weigh heavily in the development of the self.

What I have attempted thus far is to provide a model of the genesis of the self which focuses on how the sense of self and object-self relate to the possibility of self-determination. This perspective suggests that, at least in certain social-historical settings, a self can and does arise that has the capacity for self-determination. The model presupposes the existence of a social system that is sufficiently complex and diverse to include a wealth of roles and novel behaviors, the learning of which generates a sophisticated form of sociality. Although all societies must socialize individuals into roles, the question of whether all societies are sufficiently diverse for the consciousness of living in sociality to yield a sense of self cannot be answered here. All I presume, and must presume, for my account

---

1. In this chapter the term *self* (without quotation marks) will be used when it is not necessary to distinguish between the object-self and the sense of self, and will often denote the individual who has the *capacity* for realizing the object-self *and* the sense of self. When specifically speaking of object-self or sense of self, I will use the entire phrase and not simply the term *self*.

to be valid is that we can find a sense of self on the contemporary scene. My concern is to show how a present-day experience of self-consciousness and self-determination can be accounted for, using the conceptual categories and tools at hand. This, of course, is not to denigrate the worth of projects utilizing anthropological and historical material; such material is simply outside the scope of this work.

I have been attempting to show how the socially mediated self can become a mediating self, one that actively engages in the task of self-determination. What is necessary for such a self to develop is not only the awareness of oneself as an object-self, but as an object that can be (and is) superseded in the lived experience of the sense of self. One must come to live as a function of one's sociality, the not-self (the lack that is present to consciousness), in order to be able to alter the object-self.

But have I not made the process of development leading to self-determination appear to be too "natural" and direct? Clearly, the self is subject to the vicissitudes of a prolonged period of dependence on others, and during this period there are numerous ways in which the process of development can be short-circuited. One does not have to be a Freudian to acknowledge that the long period of dependence during infancy and early childhood leaves the human being a creature especially sensitive to the other. We have discussed the power of others in terms of prohibitions, and the tension they give rise to when in conflict with various impulses. Yet the other is at first, after all, the caretaker who regularly reinforces certain types of behavior.[2] Children take on certain behaviors and roles because there are those present who value these behaviors and roles. The content of these roles and behaviors surely matters in influencing the development of the self, and one can find numerous situations in which the content of the object-self impedes the growth of self-determination.

To be somewhat more specific, suppose that the social system in

2. See Chodorow, *The Reproduction of Mothering*, for a neo-Freudian analysis of how differences in male and female child-rearing lead to the continued subordination of women. I should mention here that I in no way deny the existence of differences that foster the subservience of women. As a matter of fact, my account in the following pages will provide reasons for why this is indeed an acceptable hypothesis. But I do have serious disagreements with the Freudian perspective, as will become apparent in the last section of this chapter.

which a child matures not only prohibits specific acts, but severely restricts any show of negativity on the part of the individual. I have in mind here, for example, an extremely hierarchical society in which there is a slave class or a class equivalent to, let us say, the untouchables in India, or a family setting in which certain members are treated as the psychological equivalent of slaves. The roles that such selves come to take are not interchangeable, in that the slave cannot play the role of master. The self develops solely as an object-self, for whom the power of the no has been in one direction only, that is, from the other so as to delimit one as an object-self. As a slave, literally or metaphorically, one is consigned primarily to one role, or a limited set of roles, and to experiencing much of the world as not-self, as other. One is thereby conditioned to live a circumscribed existence. In not having learned how to negate aspects of the world and one's own object-self that the consciousness of the sense of self has grown accustomed to negating, one remains what the other has made one, an object. While some slaves in this sense may succeed in learning the power of the no, there is certainly a developmental handicap for those who find themselves dominated by others. A social setting that actually has a limited number of roles available or one that works to limit the availability of roles for large segments of the populace (thereby minimizing diversity and novelty), creates many an obstacle to arriving at a self-determining self.

Although I have argued that it is the other and the social world in general that make possible the development of self-determination, it is clear that the other(s) and the social-economic system can also inhibit and prevent the realization of such a self. My goal here is not to outline all the possible ways in which this end can be either realized or short-circuited, but to explore a critical type of obstacle and a way to overcome it. The obstacle I speak of is the relationship of dominance versus subordinance.

To become actively self-determining, one must either have been, or be recognized as, capable of autonomy; one must have been responded to as a person and not merely as an object-self. This is to say something more than what Kant says, namely, that persons should be treated not solely as means but also as ends in themselves, or that all persons are entitled to respect by virtue of their basic rationality. It is to say that if we mean by freedom the capac-

ity for self-determination, then my individual freedom depends on
the other, and not only because the other has the power to prevent
or prohibit me from acting as I wish. Rather, being (self-) conscious
that *I* wish, and can act on this wish, is a function of the intersub-
jective relationships in which the self develops and lives.

Or, in the terms that we have been using until now, the transition
from object-self to the sense of self requires the presence of the
negative as limit, as well as a social context that does not continually reduce the self to the status of an object—an object-self that
experiences the not-self as external to self, as that which is wholly
other. In other words, as but an object-self, the negative, which is
a qualitative limit, never comes to be seen as a property of my being
that I can utilize to negate the not-self. I do not experience the not-
self as my personal lack, because the lack remains out there, in the
world, a region that I must not transgress. It is the beyond. I become merely a living thing among other things, a quasi-in-itself
surrounded by what I am not, a being that perceives itself to be
finished, complete. I see myself as incapable of changing except by
becoming the other and losing whatever individuality I have come
to think of as me. A willingness to change under such circumstances may require a severe threat to my body, to the biological
existence on which I seem to depend, because other forces for
change appear to threaten the only me that I have, that is, the comfortable object-self.

We will address the manner in which domination affects the development of the self by drawing on Hegel's master–slave dialectic.
Since the first publication of *Phenomenology of Spirit* in 1807, this
dialectic has influenced and been used—and perhaps abused—by
a number of the most prominent and well-known thinkers of our
era, from Marx to Sartre (whose analysis of the look is heavily
indebted to it). The commentaries have been numerous, sometimes
even brilliant, and I have no intention of even attempting to provide
the definitive commentary here. My goal is simply to take a text
that directly relates to the topic at hand and reinterpret it to fit the
model I have been developing. For those readers not familiar with
Hegel's text, I ask that you not think of this analysis as Hegel's, but
one which modifies the direction of his original dialectic, if for no
other reason than that it alters the dialectic by abstracting it from
the *Phenomenology of Spirit*. Nevertheless, I am convinced that the

following secular social-psychological reading of Hegel's dialectic complements his version by asking questions which Hegel did not ask, and would not have asked, given the "spirit of his times." Yet, they need to be addressed.

Self-consciousness and the Master–Slave Dialectic

In order to explore how the relationship of master and slave affects the development of the self, we must first look at Hegel's context. The master–slave dialectic is located within the section of the *Phenomenology of Spirit* entitled "Self-consciousness," and it evolves from the struggle of the self, which is becoming conscious of itself, to remain a unified consciousness.[3] As a self becomes self-conscious, a rift occurs between the developing object-self, which consciousness is becoming increasingly aware of and fixated on, and the rest of the world in which consciousness finds itself. Hegel tells us that this emerging self-consciousness desires, and what it desires is to be made whole (again). In Freudian terms, there is an urge to recapture the feelings that existed at the stage of primary narcissism, when otherness was absent. In its quest for unity, self-consciousness seeks to negate, or deny, the existence of objects that exist independently of itself. If there are no independent others, if there is no otherness, then I will be whole again, as I was before the appearance of the object-self and the world. That which violates me by confronting me as independent must be negated.

One strategy for dealing with this otherness is consumption. The self consumes the other, digests the other, removes its otherness by incorporating it into itself. The burgeoning self-consciousness longs to become independent of (external) nature by making the entire world its own nature. Incorporating the other, however, only leads to further dependence on and acknowledgment of the other, for there must be the other to incorporate.

Long before there is an object-self, the world impinges on the infant's primary narcissism in the form of not having needs met. Perhaps it is during this stage that the consumption of objects takes precedence over any other means of denying otherness, so that (Hegel's account notwithstanding) the strategy of consumption begins before the experience of disunity in self-consciousness. Be that as it

3. Hegel, *Phenomenology of Spirit*, pp. 104–38.

may, the desire for reunification that expresses itself in negativity directed at the world in Hegel's account, expresses itself in the child's use of no at a later stage in his or her development.

In the earliest days of the primitive object-self, the world intrudes in the form of prohibitions. In order to overcome this otherness, the young child makes use of the verbal gesture no. We have seen that this stage of no-saying must, in part, give way to an identification with the prohibitions of the caretaker, so that the child can avoid living in a condition of perpetual tension. But, at first, as the nascent object-self is beginning to form, and before identification with the other takes precedence over impulse, the child struggles against the intrusion of the other. It says no to the other, again and again, often seemingly saying no for the perverse pleasure of being contrary. But there is no perverse pleasure here. The child is waging a war to preserve itself as a whole being—a war that it must eventually lose. The no has entered consciousness, and the child has no option but to learn to deal with negativity.

In Hegel's dialectic, the inability to gain satisfaction through the negation of otherness leads to a conflict between self and other. The developing self-consciousness comes up against another self-consciousness that is also seeking to declare him or her self the (apparently) independent, unified being of the non-self-conscious state. Both desire to be the independent one, the one for whom there is no otherness, and each views the other as a threat to this independence. Further, since Hegel is speaking here of an adult consciousness, he wants to say that the idea of being recognized as a self-consciousness, as that which has risen above the non-human in nature, plays a crucial role in the interaction between consciousnesses when they meet. "Unlike animals, [human beings] . . . imperiously desire to be recognized as self-consciousnesses, as something raised above purely animal life."[4]

The developing self-consciousness cannot tolerate the disunity that growing self-awareness brings, but neither can it tolerate being regarded merely as a natural "thing." It wants the wholeness of not

4. Jean Hyppolite, *Genesis and Structure of Hegel's Phenomenology of Spirit*, p. 169. This translation uses the word *men* to refer to those who seek recognition, whereas, to avoid sexist language, I have used *human beings*. (Hyppolite introduces the passage with *Les hommes* in the original.) I should also note that throughout the chapter the non-sexist language is my own, not Hegel's.

interacting with or depending on that which it takes to be other, while it shuns the unity that is provided through thinghood. In Sartre's terms, the for-itself realizes its difference from the in-itself and wishes to remain a for-itself while having the unity of an in-itself. This is clearly impossible, for the for-itself, as (self-) consciousness, is separated from itself by virtue of being consciousness.

Self-consciousness "feels" outside itself in Hegel's dialectic, and in order to be whole, this alienation must be negated. When a self-consciousness meets another self-consciousness, the first self-consciousness believes that it can recapture its unity by negating the otherness that it experiences as having its source in the other self-consciousness, while the second self-consciousness believes the same. To make matters more complicated, we know that these two share the same mode of being, that is, they are self-consciousness. They could conceivably recognize each other as having the unique being of self-consciousness, which is different from all else in nature, but, instead, even when the other speaks—and thereby declares his or her uniqueness in relation to other things by appearing to share a mode of being similar to the first—this is seen by the first consciousness only as evidence of his or her being outside of him or her self. The other speaks with the voice I alone should speak with. I have become alienated. This alien voice must be negated if I am to negate my otherness. Since each believes this, a struggle to the death ensues.[5]

Though each burgeoning self-consciousness wants to believe that it has risen above biological life, that "it is not attached to life," it cannot gain its wish by either killing or dying.[6] The reality is that "death is the *natural* negation of consciousness, negation without independence, which thus remains without the required significance of recognition."[7] To die is to become a thing; hence it would not provide consciousness with what it actually wishes, that is, to

5. I might also add that in the section of the *Phenomenology* under consideration, Hegel addresses the rise of self-consciousness in general, so that in some form the elements of this rise must be a part of each self-conscious individual's development. When he discusses an actual "battle to the death," it is clear that he is speaking about a time prior to civil society and the state. See his *Philosophy of Mind*, p. 172, par. 432, Zusatz.

6. Hegel, *Phenomenology of Spirit*, p. 113.

7. Ibid., p. 114; original emphasis.

be recognized as the independent being it takes itself to be. Becoming self-conscious creates disunity, by splitting the object(s) of consciousness from the consciousness aware of the object, and by making consciousness aware that it is apart from the world. But it also gives rise to a being that can be aware of its own unique being as self-consciousness, and, hence, different from all the rest of nature. Self-consciousness desires to be recognized for its uniqueness and must survive as a biological organism if this is to come to pass. The other must also live if there is to be one who can recognize the first self-consciousness.

Hegel declares that the self-consciousness that is prepared to die for the conviction that it is above the merely natural becomes the master, and that the master rules the self-consciousness that is not prepared to die, the slave. The slave trembles before the one who has the power of life and death; and the master has this power precisely because he or she does not fear death. The master is the being for whom ideals matter more than biological life itself and is seen as the essential in life by both him or her self and the slave. The slave is viewed as the inessential, similar to a thing, unprepared to risk biological life to rise above the animal or natural world.

What, then, are the connections between Hegel's account of the development of self-consciousness and the evolving object-self of the child? In both, the experience of otherness is basic to the development of (self) consciousness; its genesis requires the other. Both Hegel's self-consciousness and the child attempt to use the strategy of negating that which is other in order to deny the intrusion of otherness. The child, of course, is not literally a slave; nevertheless, the child has experienced a power similar to that held by Hegel's master, a power that must be obeyed at all costs, (seemingly) a power over life and death. The child and the slave capitulate in order to live, the child by making the other into the object-self, the slave by seeing the master as the ideal in life. The master might be spoken of as the slave's ego ideal, as long as the slave believes in the master.

However, the overcoming of the other through the development of the object-self cannot be the end of the story. We know that negation, having been responsible in part for catalysing the development of the object-self, is present within consciousness as that which allows for the verbal gesture no, and as that which demarcates the object-self from what is not-self. In chapter 4 I argued that negativity is placed at the disposal of consciousness as one becomes habituated to and aware of the experience of sociality. One can learn that the relation between self and not-self is fluid, and that the not-self is not external to the self but resides in consciousness as its limit. This is not to say that one does not encounter actual external limits or barriers in life, but that many behaviors and roles that were once seen solely in terms of being not-self become a property of the self through living in sociality. One has access to roles that one is not through the lack that lies in consciousness and allows for the sense of self. In having a sense of self, I live as a detotalized totality, relating myself to the self to come through the not-self that is my current limit. How then is the development of the sense of self related to Hegel's dialectic?

In having a slave, the master has one who works upon the world in order to satisfy the master's desire(s). The desire of self-consciousness expresses itself as the wish to maintain independence in the face of otherness, and the master can remain independent of the world because the slave works upon the world to satisfy the master's needs. Thus, the master does not have to engage the world, since the slave negates that which is other and serves up what has been negated in the form in which the master wishes to receive it. Because the natural is mediated by the slave, the master can avoid contact with an alien independent nature: the slave tills the soil so that the master has food to consume, and the master is desire (seemingly) satisfied.

On the other hand, the slave works upon the world and changes it, and in changing the world is transformed in turn. Things that were once independent of the slave are re-shaped by his or her activity; they are thereby humanized. But for the master, things are merely negated all at once, as when he consumes food produced by the slave.

Work . . . is desire held in check, fleetingness staved off; in other words, work forms and shapes the thing. The negative relation to the object becomes its *form* and something *permanent*, because it is precisely for the worker that the object has independence. This *negative* middle term or the formative *activity* is at the same time the individuality or pure being-for-self of consciousness which now, in the work outside of it, acquires an element of permanence.[8]

The negative, which once existed merely as the abstract and alien no of the other, is transformed under the guidance of the slave, who now sees that negation can be re-directed toward an external object to make of it a humanized object. The independence of the human-ized object reflects the independence of the mind that shaped it. "Consciousness, *qua* worker, comes to see in the independent being [of the object] its *own* independence."[9]

The slave has lived under the power of the no of the master and trembled before this power. Hegel claims that the overcoming of this state of complete fear is found in making the negative one's own, as opposed to having it remain the abstract no that resides in the province of the other, the master.

In fashioning the thing, the bondsman's [the slave's] own negativity, his being-for-self, becomes an object for him only through his setting at nought the existing *shape* confronting him. But this objective *negative* mo-ment is none other than the alien being before which it has trembled. Now, however, he destroys this alien negative moment, posits *himself* as a nega-tive in the permanent order of things, and thereby becomes *for himself*, someone existing on his own account.[10]

The otherness of the world, confronting the slave as the realm of the negative, is negated by his or her activity; to consciously negate the negative of the not-self is to posit the negative as mine. It is to recognize oneself as a source of the negative in the order of things. It is to take that which is alien, external to oneself, and remove the externality by shaping it with one's own power.

To place Hegel's remarks more directly in line with the previous discussion of limit and sociality, we should first note that overcom-ing the "alien moment" entails realizing that the (seemingly) exter-nal limit of the object-self, that is, the not-self, exists as a modifi-able qualitative limit within the individual. Prior to this the no of the other, the prohibitions of the caretaker before which the child

8. Ibid., p. 118; original emphasis.
9. Ibid., p. 118; original emphasis; translator's insertion.
10. Ibid., p. 118; original emphasis.

trembled, were internalized as the child identified with them in the development of the object-self. The no was present, but its use against the other was moderated by the need to mollify the other. At this stage it can be said of the child in relation to the parent what Hegel says of the slave in relation to the master, that he or she "sets aside its own being-for-self, and in so doing itself does what the first does to it." [11]

In doing what the other does to it, the child builds an object-self. But in being solely an object-self, the individual does not experience the negative as its own malleable qualitative limit. The negative is merely the not-self which lies out there, in the world, as that which the self is not. We know, though, that this perception of the negative is inaccurate—even for the individual who has developed only an object-self—because that which allows there to be a limit between object-self and other is itself part of the individual. Nevertheless, such an individual will view itself exclusively in terms of the roles it has become, and the prohibitions that it has accepted, so long as the not-self is seen to be outside the (object-) self. It is at this juncture that Hegel has the slave "rescued" by work, for in working, the negative manifests its being-for the individual as part of the individual. To follow Hegel here, I would have to say that in the transition from object-self to the sense of self, a source must be found that allows the negative to be known as one's own.

How does one actively take hold of the negative? One might look to the power over things that the child experiences in the mastery of new tasks, and this would parallel the slave's work in Hegel's account. I do not doubt the importance of the mastery of tasks, but this mastery does not arise in a social vacuum. In addition to the importance of novelty, the availability of numerous and complex roles, and the mastery of tasks, there is another key factor in the development of the sense of self. *Recognition* is central to the master–slave dialectic and to rising above the circumscribed object-self.

Domination and Recognition

The master, as we have seen, once exhibited desire—the desire of self-consciousness to be whole, to be without otherness—which arose when consciousness became separated from itself and the

11. Ibid., p. 116.

world. The master now appears to be desire satisfied, for he or she has the slave to remove the otherness of things, to humanize them, and can enjoy them without having to acknowledge their ubiquitous presence, which is to say, that he has the slave to mediate his relationship to nature, to things.

For the lord . . . the *immediate* relation becomes through this mediation [that is, the slave's work] the sheer negation of the thing, or the enjoyment of it. What desire failed to achieve, he succeeds in doing, viz. to have done with the thing altogether, and to achieve satisfaction in the enjoyment of it. Desire failed to do this because of the thing's independence; but the lord, who has interposed the bondsman between it and himself, takes to himself only the dependent aspect of the thing and has the pure enjoyment of it.[12]

The slave recognizes the master as the essential in life. The master determines what the slave should or should not do, so that the slave (seemingly) comes to depend on the master for the course to be followed in life. The master believes that he or she has indeed achieved the recognition desired—that is, to be seen as the independent one, not only by him or her self, but also by the other. However, authentic recognition is not possible under these circumstances, for we find that the master not only depends on the slave for recognition—and is not the independent one he or she takes him or her self to be—but that the recognition which the slave can provide must in itself remain unsatisfying. It cannot satisfy because it comes from one who has been labeled and viewed, by both master and slave, as inessential and thinglike. Recognition from one who is seen as unworthy of providing recognition is mere adulation.

Hegel's insight here is readily apparent in the most ordinary of day-to-day relationships with others. As a worker, artist, philosopher, or whatever, one desires to be recognized as a human being who masters and executes tasks, who relates to others, who is a self worthy of dignity and respect. What I wish to have is recognition from those who are themselves worthy of recognition, those I regard as peers, and to be satisfied with less is to look to those who have no knowledge or understanding of my uniqueness to render judgment on it. To be satisfied with less requires either that I dupe

12. Ibid., p. 116; original emphasis.

myself in my estimation of the capacities of those who are judging me or that I accept the recognition of those who cannot in fact provide it by assuming that this is all that recognition entails, thereby reducing it to adulation. Relationships of the master–slave type fail to win what those who promote them so often desire, recognition and independence, for the master depends on the slave for a recognition that the slave cannot authentically provide, given the parameters of the relationship.

In Hegel's words, "for recognition proper the moment is lacking, that what the lord does to the other he also does to himself, and what the bondsman does to himself he should also do to the other. The outcome is a recognition that is one-sided and unequal." [13]

Hierarchical situations of this variety promote what I would call pseudo-recognition, since one cannot be genuinely recognized by an other when one has a false image of self and other. To accept pseudo-recognition as if it were genuine recognition can be seen as a form of bad faith, for, although claiming to be this individual to oneself, one is not the individual who is thus recognized. It is to take the lack, the not-self that lies before consciousness, and to fill it artificially by magically converting the possible (self) into the real.

Yet the acceptance of pseudo-recognition need not be due to bad faith. Bad faith presupposes a self that has a sense of self, one that appreciates the possible as its own. But there is the acceptance of pseudo-recognition that stems from not knowing who one is or what one can become. Ignorance of this sort locks the self into being solely an object-self and is often fostered by masters wishing to perpetuate servitude. The slave is "forced" to believe the master's myth, the myth that he or she not only is, but must remain, a dependent consciousness. Sartre, in *Being and Nothingness*, does not allow for ignorance of this sort, because he defines consciousness in such a manner that it is found ready-made with its freedom, and any claim of ignorance is seen as an excuse, a flight from freedom. But if the early Sartre had understood that the sense of self is itself a product of a developmental process, and as such is not an inevitable property of consciousness, then he would have had to modify his most basic claims regarding freedom and bad faith. The power

13. Ibid., p. 116.

to lock the self into objecthood, into the servitude of being only an object-self that presumes it has little power over the possible, stems from the manner in which the development of the self lends itself to being arrested at the level of object-self.[14] How so?

The self as an object-self is a mediated being. One does not come to have an object-self unless there are others whose behaviors and roles one takes and makes one's own. We have seen that in the development of the self various prohibitions are internalized, and that the object-self comes into being, in part, through the no of the other. Having now introduced the notion of recognition, the previous comparison of Hegel's slave with the developing child must come to include the following: the slave, living in pseudo-recognition, believes that he or she must depend on the master to determine his or her life; the child, on the other hand, for quite some time actually does depend on the other, the caretaker, to determine his or her life. Whereas with the master and the slave, we have assumed that there is at least an object-self present (thereby allowing for the possibility of pseudo-recognition), with the child, we are dealing with an object-self that is only in the process of developing, and in this development, recognition by the caretaker is critical. The adult can live a lie by accepting pseudo-recognition. With the child the object-self is so fluid that the danger is not one of pseudo-recognition, but of a lack of recognition that may pre-

---

14. In a rather Sartrean fashion, Martin Buber emphasizes the importance of courage for an authentic existence. "The widespread tendency to live from the recurrent impression one makes instead of from the steadiness of one's being is not a 'nature.' It originates, in fact, on the other side of the interhuman life itself, in men's dependence upon one another. It is no light thing to be confirmed in one's being by others, and seeming [that is, appearing a certain way] deceptively offers itself as a help in this. To yield to seeming is man's essential cowardice, to resist it is his essential courage" (*The Knowledge of Man—A Philosophy of the Interhuman,* p. 78). This is taken from an essay entitled "Elements of the Interhuman." Buber, of course, is much more concerned with the interhuman and with mutuality than the early Sartre, and he sees our relationships with others not primarily in terms of conflict, but as necessary to becoming authentic selves. Nevertheless, Buber's understanding of cowardice and courage implies the presence of freedom, a presence he is not entitled to assume. The notions of cowardice and courage are only appropriate for a (fully) responsible self, one that has had the opportunity to view itself as more than an object-self and to be confirmed in this viewing in a way that it becomes an active part of the self's life. The sense of self neither arises *ex nihilo* nor comes to appreciate its own power without the aid of the other.

vent crystallization of the qualities and characteristics that define the developing object-self.

In order to understand just how basic recognition is to the object-self's development, we must recall the importance of cognition in the development of Mead's object-self. To have an object-self one must not only come to take the role of the other but must also be able to respond and view the role from the perspective of the other. In other words, one takes a role and then comes to know this role by making it into an object. The object is viewed from a certain perspective, which has also arisen from the other, according to Mead. Being able to view myself from the perspective of the other is crucial to the development of my object-self, and when the other recognizes me, I am made aware of myself. I am brought to see myself as the other sees me. Further, we can say that recognition by the other is a form of *re-cognition,* that is, a form of awareness in which I am not only aware-of but confirmed in my awareness of the object-self I have come to take myself to be. Re-cognition is directly linked to self-consciousness; it is the mirror by and through which I confirm my own object-self, by being conscious of it through the eyes of the other. Given that the child's world is shot through with contingency, if the other fails to recognize him or her through this look of recognition, then he or she has lost a crucial source of information regarding who or what the object-self is.

Consider Mead's notion of the generalized other. For the object-self to be whole, it must come to reflect the integration of the generalized other, which for Mead can be seen as a product of society as a whole. But the development of the societal generalized other for each individual must result from interaction with particular individuals, individuals who are initially caretakers. If the child does not receive recognition for taking the attitudes, roles or behaviors that go to make up the generalized other, the seeing of the object-self from the perspective of the other becomes short-circuited, so to speak, and the re-cognition of the object-self from the perspective of society's generalized other never really happens. One cannot properly "watch" oneself, which means that the object-self—depending as it does on the shaping and ordering influence of observation—never reaches the level of integration one would expect if the child could take the perspective of the generalized other.[15] One

15. Cf. ch. 1 above.

can also say that the generalized other depends on the individual's capacity to abstract from the "game" of society certain "rules" that are implicit in it, and that the child needs to be recognized as he or she begins to formulate these rules in order that their validity may be confirmed. If the other fails to recognize me during the formation of the object-self, in a very fundamental way I am not, for as yet I have no object-self apart from my interaction with others.

The reader may be wondering at this point how it is that, on the one hand, I can claim that pseudo-recognition is what characterizes hierarchical relationships of the master and slave variety, and, on the other, speak of the importance to the child of the caretaker's recognition. After all, what could be more hierarchical than the relationship of caretaker to child?

However, it is not solely because it is hierarchical that the master–slave relationship promotes pseudo-recognition; rather, it is because of the nature of this particular hierarchy, which does not allow either person in the relationship to recognize the other for what he or she truly is, to recognize that the master is not the independent one nor the slave the totally dependent one. This said, I now wish to qualify the above by noting that it is possible for the master and slave to recognize certain specific qualities in the other without disavowing the dominance-subservience relationship; for example, both may be excellent horseback riders and recognize each other as such. Turning once more to the caretaker–child relationship, it is by definition hierarchical, so that a recognition in which each recognizes the other as fundamentally a peer is impossible. Nevertheless, the caretaker can recognize specific qualities, characteristics, behaviors, and roles of the child because the caretaker possesses the roles and behaviors for which the child is being recognized—for example, parenting behavior in which the child takes care of a doll. The caretaker is recognizing the child for behaviors and roles that the caretaker can claim as his or her own; therefore, this does not yield pseudo-recognition. However, to use an extreme example, if the caretaker looked to the child for recognition as a great writer or artist, the recognition so provided would be only pseudo-recognition.

In terms of the sense of self, the importance of being recognized for specific skills, behaviors, and roles by others who possess these attributes, pales in contrast to being recognized as a person who can make judgments regarding his or her own future. As a matter of fact, one might view someone who only acknowledges specific behaviors and roles of the other in narcissistic terms, for he or she recognizes the other only insofar as the other is like him or her. *Mutual recognition,* on the other hand, entails more than the recognition of the other for certain behaviors or roles, however important the latter may be in the child's development and for the adult's concept of (object-) self. In mutual recognition I see the other as entitled to confirmation as a person. I see the other as other, as one who has a future of his or her own, yet as one who is related to me in having a sense of self. The caretaker who assumes that the child can, and should, become self-determining looks to recognize actions of the child that are conducive to independence, with the expectation that someday he or she will stand, not hierarchically related to the caretaker, but related in mutual recognition.

The dependence on the other for recognition is as old as the object-self itself and continues in varying degrees into adulthood. This provides the other with a unique power. If the other does not wish the dependence to end, he or she can refuse to recognize any "addition" to the self that might promote independence. This is a primordial refusal of recognition in a certain sense, in that one is not only not being recognized for a specific quality or attribute, but is not being recognized as an individual capable of having a self that can come to direct its own development. The self is prevented from gaining independence by not being recognized as one who can come to contain and determine his or her own limit, as one who is entitled to own the negative. One is not recognized as having the potential for a sense of self.

The self lives in novelty and sociality, and out of this can arise a sense of self, assuming that one has first been provided with sufficient consistency and recognition to develop an object-self. Once the sense of self arises, negation can be turned against an old object-self as consciousness realizes a new self. This ability to shape a new self requires that I know that the power of the negative is mine to direct. The slave comes to be independent by shaping the world and by seeing his or her own independence reflected in the thing shaped. In the social world of the child, what he or she can shape first and foremost is the other; but for this shaping of the other to have reality, the other must recognize the legitimacy of the child's no-saying. This takes place in the acknowledgment of the child's impact on the other, when the other responds to the child's no by heeding it. If the other does not recognize this no, does not respond to it as the prerogative of the child (that is, recognizes only its own accepted norms and ways of proceeding), the no remains alien for the child. The child lives in a world in which the negative is an external law, a law that circumscribes and proscribes and in the end prevents self-creation.

In becoming an object-self, one internalizes certain patterns of behavior and excludes others. To be an object-self entails *not* being *x, y,* or *z.* For the (object-) self that is not linked to a sense of self, that does not know how to determine itself, *x, y,* or *z* are seen as totally unrelated to itself—as alien, foreign, other to the core. This object-self is enclosed by itself. It shuns the novel. It shuns its sociality in order to protect itself as an object-self from otherness. At the same time, it lives in perpetual dependence on the other, because the other has provided and continues to provide this object-self with the roles and norms that make up its life. It looks to the other to recognize its roles, and its norms reflect the generalized other. This object-self perpetually mirrors itself in the generalized other in order to be, so that threats to the (generalized) other are viewed as threats to its survival as a self. Change would mean an end to recognition, the recognition it receives from the all-important generalized other through specific others.

I wish to emphasize that this account should be viewed as a model, and that, like all models, it abstracts from concrete individuals and relationships. In the preceding paragraph, for example, we discussed the "self-enclosed" object-self, but in fact selves are rarely so completely self-enclosed. But a model of this sort does, in all its skeletal abstraction, assist in illuminating the development of the self and seeing how this development can be obstructed. However, at this juncture, it would seem advisable to clarify the model as a whole by comparing it with an approach to development that is well known, one to which we have already referred, and with which it shares certain affinities, while differing at crucial points. That approach is Freud's, specifically his claims regarding the relationship of aggression to the formation of the superego.

In Contrast to Freud—A Final Summation

By the time he came to write *Civilization and its Discontents,* Freud had become convinced that "the meaning of the evolution of civilization is no longer obscure to us. It must present the struggle between Eros and Death, between the instinct of life and the instinct of destruction, as it works itself out in the human species." [16]

Given that each human being possesses (or is possessed by) a certain amount of love and aggressivity, we can understand human interactions as a struggle between these two forces. Civilization, as the handmaid of Eros, cannot tolerate unrestrained manifestations of aggressivity, and so the aggressivity of individuals must be curbed in some way. The curbing of this aggressivity entails its redirection, from outward against the world to inward against the individual.

His aggressiveness is introjected, internalized; it is, in point of fact, sent back to where it came from—that is, it is directed towards his own ego. There it is taken over by a portion of the ego, which sets itself over against the rest of the ego as super-ego, and which now, in the form of 'conscience,' is ready to put into action against the ego the same harsh aggressiveness that the ego would have liked to satisfy upon other, extraneous individuals. [17]

We have within us an outpost of the other, the superego, to prevent us from violating what the other, civilization, deems correct. The weapon of the other is the guilt we suffer when we think to violate the other. The more hostile we are toward the other, the more aggressivity we must contain; the more we wish to let our impulses run rampant, the more we must punish ourselves. The superego is the realm of the other that has become our own domain. It is the night watchman who never sleeps. "It is simply a continuation of the severity of the external authority, to which it has succeeded and which it has in part replaced." [18]

But is the degree of aggressivity toward oneself due to the severity of the external authority's demands or to the quantity of aggressivity possessed by the individual as an organic endowment? The answer for Freud, of course, is that both are factors. We can more fully understand how these two factors operate in the same individual if we note the original derivation of the superego. Freud tells us that a great deal of hostility is generated toward those who

16. Freud, *Civilization and its Discontents*, p. 69.
17. Ibid., p. 70.
18. Ibid., p. 74.

first force the organism to renounce its drives or urges. However, the child is not in a position to allow this aggressivity to affect the other, not only because the other is all-powerful, but because he or she loves the other. The child finds his or her way out of this situation by identifying with the other, introjecting the other.

By means of identification he takes the unattackable authority into himself. The authority now turns into his super-ego and enters into possession of all the aggressiveness which a child would have liked to exercise against it. . . . The relationship between the super-ego and the ego is a return, distorted by a wish, of the real relationships between the ego, as yet undivided, and an external object.[19]

The amount of aggressivity possessed by the individual as an organic endowment combines with the severity of the internalized demands of the other to produce varying degrees of superego vengefulness. Further, it should be noted, it is often the loving parent or the lenient parent who appears loving, according to Freud, who contributes to raising an overly anxious and guilt-ridden child, because such a child is prevented from manifesting aggressivity outward: "Apart from a constitutional factor . . . a severe conscience arises from the joint operation of two factors: the frustration of instinct, which unleashes aggressiveness, and the experience of being loved, which turns the aggressiveness inwards and hands it over to the super-ego."[20] Much of Freud's vision for escape from the pain of neurosis entails the weakening or replacement of an overly burdensome superego with a more tolerant one.

As I have noted several times, when combined with Mead's concept of taking the role of the other, Freud's concept of identification is a valuable one for helping to explain the development of the object-self. But I disagree with a great deal in his account of the formation of the superego. First, I assume no equivalent to the all-pervasive instincts, or drives, of love and death.[21] I have spoken of

19. Ibid., p. 76.
20. Ibid., p. 77n.
21. Bruno Bettelheim argues in his recent work *Freud and Man's Soul* (pp. 103–12), that the German term *Trieb* can, and should, be translated as impulse or drive, since Freud wishes to distinguish the more malleable impulses or drives of human beings from the instincts of animals. There is much merit in this suggestion; however, bowing to tradition, I will use the term *instinct* while also providing an alternative.

impulse, having in mind those urges or needs originally dictated by our biological endowment and satisfied through certain stimuli, for example, hunger for food, the urge to be touched and held, the preference for certain forms of sensory stimulation.[22] In other words, I have not wished to suggest by the word *impulse* anything quite so far-reaching as Freud's two basic instincts or drives, which, in the later Freud, become principles for organizing reality. Nevertheless, I do assume that human beings have impulses that are originally of a biological nature, and that these are subject to extensive modification and transformation as they come under the influence of social interaction.

While there are similarities between my use of the concept of negation and Freud's concept of aggression, the two concepts have fundamentally different derivations. What Freud terms *aggression* is organically derived (albeit culturally fashioned). I have argued that negation, as a socially derived component of the mind, is internalized and have claimed that it is in the frustration of impulses due to prohibitions that negation enters consciousness. One identifies with the no of the other in order to overcome the no, to make it one's own. This parallels Freud's account of how the child curbs its own hostility by introjecting the prohibition of the other, thereby forming the superego. But aggression does not wait on the social for its derivation, it is a given of human nature (and perhaps cosmic nature), whereas the role of negation in my account, while it relates to the curbing of impulses, is not that of an impulse or instinct.

Without positing an instinct or drive of death, of aggressivity, it is still possible to explain the self-destruction that occurs when the negative (aggressivity for Freud) is not allowed to be directed outward. When the caretaker says no, this no may be internalized as a specific prohibition, for example, not to eat cookies. But it may also be internalized as a non-specific abstraction, that is, as the verbal gesture no. By complying with the prohibition of the caretaker, the child is met with approval; hence, the child can disarm the other and at the same time be reinforced for doing so. Prohibitions thus internalized act as ideals to be met and followed (in Freud's terms

22. For Mead's definition of *impulse*, and why he prefers to use this term rather than *instinct*, see ch. 4, n. 9 above.

they come to make up one's ego ideal, or superego). Failure to live up to them gives rise to anxiety and guilt. But most children do more than merely succumb to the no of the other; they come to use it and make it their own, so as, for example, to resist the caretaker's no. But if the negative is only directed at the child, so that the no that could meet the other and refuse the other's wishes is not allowed to manifest itself, what happens is that the child receives a profoundly confusing message: "I (the caretaker) say no to you, and you learn to say no as a verbal gesture. You may expect that in using the no, as you use other verbal gestures, you will be rewarded for its use. However, every time you say no, I will again say no to you." Under such circumstances, the no is directed back at the individual, as Freud's aggressivity is directed back, and the child is rewarded for not asserting him or her self in the face of the other. To challenge the other, or to think of challenging the other, brings the no back to oneself, and guilt and anxiety warn one not to overstep one's bounds. The no, then, acts to delimit the self by enclosing it within a world of the not-self, and this not-self remains other, alien, so that whatever object-self one has is rigidly circumscribed. Under these circumstances the no is but a shield that is used against anything foreign, that is, what has not been accepted by the other, the other who has molded the object-self. The no is now a deformed qualitative limit, for although it is part of the organism, it is under the control of the other, and one uses it against one's (possible) self.

Even if it were true that parents who are loving or who appear loving tend to produce anxious children, one would not have to resort to Freud's notion of aggression to account for this. One could point to the fact that anxiety is produced by, among other things, what we might loosely term the insecurity of inconsistency, and that loving, as well as hostile, parents may be inconsistent.

It might also be said paradoxically, that a loving parent who is too lenient may fail to acknowledge the no of the child sufficiently by always heeding that no. In this case the child's impact on the other is diminished because the other fails to recognize the importance of the no. The other must do more than simply heed the no; for a sense of self to emerge, the other must also provide a world for the child to affect and shape. Once the no is introduced, the repercussions are far from trivial when it is either dismissed by not allowing the child the prerogative of saying no or yielded to at every turn. In both cases there is a failure to adequately recognize the child's no after the trauma of its emergence.

The account I have been offering differs most from Freud on the question of whether a sense of self is possible. For Freud, the self remains an object-self, determined by the interaction of instincts or drives, familial relations, and societal norms. I have sought to show how the sense of self develops through sociality, and how consciousness comes to live as that which lacks, having the not-self as part of itself. The transition from object-self to this sense of self requires that the world respond to and recognize the no of the child.

But what of the unconscious? Have I not neglected what Freud would consider the most inimical thing of all to the freedom implied by the sense of self? In arguing for the existence of an object-self and, following Mead, of a generalized other, however, I have not implied that one is conscious of the totality of the object-self at each and every moment. The argument, then, is not whether there is or is not a pool of non-conscious behavioral responses (or norms, values, ideals, and so on) that can influence conscious behavior, for the existence of an object-self (and a generalized other) implies that there is. The question is whether in becoming conscious of the object-self and then becoming aware of the world as the not-self in which one participates, one can reconstitute oneself. I have not argued, like Sartre, that consciousness is free at each instant or that it is a spontaneous "nothing." But, unlike Freud, I have sought to show that consciousness comes to be provided with a knowledge of its own possibilities as the not-self becomes part of (self-) consciousness and one develops a sense of self. The object-self is not fixed permanently, because it can relate to a consciousness that has a sense of self. Though we have been, and are, determined by our past, we can come to determine how these past determinations will participate in our future. Freedom, then, is not unrestricted choice but entails the reconstitution of the object-self through the not-self as one lives in sociality.

It is true that Freud sees the therapeutic situation in terms of reconstituting the past or one's perception of the past; however, this reconstitution (for example, by decreasing the severity of the superego) is viewed only in terms of the object-self. In Freud's thinking, the object-self can be modified, but one is solely an object-self (and instincts), so that consciousness is not seen to live in a world of novelty that it can actively transform into self.

To view the self solely as an object-self is commonplace in the market economy of the modern world. In this economic system, the self is often treated merely as an object among other objects, as a commodity with certain characteristics or qualities, and is frequently understood by the science of the times to be a collection of behaviors, instincts, and so on. In an environment of this sort it is not difficult to understand how the need for recognition of one's qualities, which are the source of (object) selfhood, can lead to a quest for fame at any price. Fame, however, distorts the potential for the sense of self by solely acknowledging qualities or characteristics of the self; that is, it allows only for the object-self, and often trivializes even that.

Of course, the situation is somewhat more complicated than the above would suggest, for we are also taught that we are free to choose and make of ourselves whatever we wish. Both the reduction of the self to an object and the insistence that the individual is completely free in making all decisions seriously distort the nature of the self and self-determination. Recognition of developmental complexity gives way to the assumption, on the one hand, that one rather miraculously becomes responsible for one's decisions at a certain age—perhaps because one is endowed with a soul that possesses free will—and, on the other, that one is only a microcosm of the social, an object determined by the social relations that have come to constitute the (object-) self.

In mutual recognition the one-sidedness of such formulations is revealed. The self sees itself in the other and the other in the self. Our social self becomes conscious of itself and of its possibilities. Yet, to the degree that one lives as a circumscribed object-self, one is recognized only for qualities and characteristics, not as the keeper of the self and not-self, not as a potentially self-determining being. To recognize the other only in this manner is ultimately a form of narcissism. It is a narcissism in which I do not recognize the other as both similar and different from myself, as one who can shape the world in an unfamiliar fashion; I recognize the other only because the other is a reflection of my own object-self, that is, of a quality or characteristic of myself. Mutual recognition, on the other hand, entails the seeing of the self in the other while, at the same time, the other remains other and sees me in the same fashion.

Sartre's account of the look presupposes selves that view themselves as object-selves. However, if when I look at the other, I recognize in him or her the capacity for developing a self-determining consciousness, then my look does not transform the other into an object but assists in the liberation of the other from objecthood. Of course, if I and the other have come to fear otherness and meet as but object-selves, then when I am looked-at by the other I may be reminded of the power that circumscribed my (object-) self and placed the not-self beyond reach. I cringe before this power, a power that views me as the object I view myself as, but with renewed immediacy and authority due to its looking directly at me as an object.

If I have lived my life as a circumscribed object-self, whose sense of self has either not developed or been severely restricted, I will seek to nurture my object-self on the limited recognition provided by those who are the leaders of society, for they symbolically embody the (generalized) other that has constituted me. To escape being a slave to the recognition of these others—which denies me my potential and locks me into being merely an object among other objects—I must come to embrace the negative as my own. This is precisely why it is so important that the caretaker recognize the negative as belonging to the child during the child's development. Yet it is also clear that if the caretaker thinks of him or her self as primarily an object-self, he or she will expect the child to be the same with regard to the capacities of the self and will thus be unable to provide the necessary recognition. The breaking of this vicious circle is the work of those who not only know that self-determination is possible, being neither a miraculous nor solely fortuitous occurrence, but also understand the difficulties entailed in its realization.

Bibliography

Aboulafia, Mitchell. "Engels, Darwin, and Hegel's Idea of Contingency." *Studies in Soviet Thought* 21 (1980):211–19.

———. "From Domination to Recognition." In *Beyond Domination: New Perspectives on Women and Philosophy,* edited by Carol C. Gould, pp. 175–85. Totowa, N.J.: Rowman and Allanheld, 1984.

———. *The Self-Winding Circle: A Study of Hegel's System.* Modern Concepts of Philosophy, series founding editor Marvin Farber. St. Louis: W. H. Green, 1982.

Ames, Van Meter. "Mead and Sartre on Man." *Journal of Philosophy* 53 (1956):205–19.

Beauvoir, Simone de. *The Second Sex.* Translated by H. M. Parshley. New York: Alfred A. Knopf, 1953. Reprint, New York: Vintage Books, 1974.

Bergoffen, Debra B. "Sartre's Transcendence of the Ego: a Methodological Reading." *Philosophy Today* 22 (1978):244–51.

Bettelheim, Bruno. *Freud and Man's Soul.* New York: Alfred A. Knopf, 1983.

Buber, Martin. *I and Thou.* Translated by Walter Kaufmann. New York: Scribners, 1970.

———. *The Knowledge of Man—A Philosophy of the Interhuman.* Translated by M. Friedman and R. G. Smith. Edited by M. Friedman. New York: Harper and Row, Torchbooks, 1966.

Catalano, Joseph S. *A Commentary on Jean-Paul Sartre's "Being and Nothingness."* New York: Harper and Row, 1974. Reprint, Chicago: University of Chicago Press, 1980.

Chodorow, Nancy. *The Reproduction of Mothering: Psychoanalysis and the Sociology of Gender.* Berkeley: University of California Press, 1978.

Dreyfus, Herbert L., and Hoffman, Piotr. "Sartre's Changed Conception of Consciousness: From Lucidity to Opacity." In *The Philosophy of Jean-Paul Sartre, Library of Living Philosophers, Vol. XVI,* edited by Paul Arthur Schilpp, pp. 229–45. La Salle, Illinois: Open Court, 1981.

Freud, Sigmund. *Beyond the Pleasure Principle.* Standard Edition, vol. 18. London: Hogarth Press and Institute of Psycho-Analysis, 1955. Translated and edited by James Strachey. Reprint, with introduction by Gregory Zilboorg. New York: W. W. Norton, 1961.

———. *Civilization and its Discontents.* Standard Edition, vol. 21. London: Hogarth Press and Institute of Psycho-Analysis, 1961. Translated and edited by James Strachey. Reprint, New York: W. W. Norton, 1962.

———. *The Ego and the Id.* Standard Edition, vol. 19. London: Hogarth Press and Institute of Psycho-Analysis, 1961. Translated by Joan Riviere. Revised and edited by James Strachey. Reprint, New York: W. W. Norton, 1962.

———. *A General Introduction to Psychoanalysis.* Translated by Joan Riviere. Preface by Ernest Jones and G. Stanley Hall. New York: Pocket Books, 1953.

———. *Group Psychology and the Analysis of the Ego.* Standard Edition, vol. 18. London: Hogarth Press and Institute of Psycho-Analysis, 1955. Translated and edited by James Strachey. Reprint, New York: W. W. Norton, 1959.

———. "On Narcissism: An Introduction." In *Collected Papers,* vol. 4, translated by Joan Riviere, pp. 30–59. New York: Basic Books, 1959.

Gould, Carol C. *Marx's Social Ontology.* Cambridge: MIT Press, 1978.

Hegel, G. W. F. *Logic, Being Part One of the Encyclopaedia of the Philosophical Sciences.* 1830. Translated by W. Wallace. Foreword by J. N. Findlay. Oxford: Oxford University Press, 1975.

———. *Phenomenology of Spirit.* Translated by A. V. Miller, with analysis of the text and Foreword by J. N. Findlay.Oxford: Oxford University Press, 1977.

———. *Philosophy of Mind, Being Part Three of the Encyclopaedia of the Philosophical Sciences.* 1830. Translated by W. Wallace, with Zusätze translated by A. V. Miller. Foreword by J. N. Findlay. Oxford: Oxford University Press, 1971.

———. *The Philosophy of Nature, Being Part Two of the Encyclopaedia of the Philosophical Sciences.* 1830. Translated by A. V. Miller. Foreword by J. N. Findlay. Oxford: Oxford University Press, 1970.

———. *Science of Logic.* Translated by A. V. Miller. Foreword by J. N. Findlay. London: George Allen and Unwin; New York: Humanities Press, 1969.

Heidegger, Martin. "What is Metaphysics?" In *Basic Writings,* edited, with an introduction, by David Farrell Krell, pp. 95–112. New York: Harper and Row, 1977.

Hyppolite, Jean. *Genesis and Structure of Hegel's Phenomenology of Spirit.* Translated by Samuel Cherniak and John Heckman. Evanston: Northwestern University Press, 1974. Original French edition: *Genèse et structure de la Phénoménologie de l'esprit de Hegel.* Paris: Aubier, Editions Montaigne, 1946.

James, William. *The Writings of William James: A Comprehensive Edition.* Edited by John J. McDermott. New York: Random House, Modern Library, 1968. Reprint, Chicago: University of Chicago Press, 1977.

Jay, Martin. *The Dialectical Imagination—A History of the Frankfurt School and the Institute of Social Research 1923–1950.* Boston: Little, Brown, 1973.

Kenevan, Phyllis Berdt. "Self-Consciousness and the Ego in the Philosophy of Sartre." In *The Philosophy of Jean-Paul Sartre, Library of Living Philosophers, Vol. XVI,* edited by Paul Arthur Schilpp, pp. 197–210. La Salle, Illinois: Open Court, 1981.

Kojève, Alexandre. *Introduction to the Reading of Hegel.* Assembled by R. Queneau. Translated by James H. Nichols, Jr. Edited by Allan Bloom. New York: Basic Books, 1969.

Laing, R. D. *The Divided Self: An Existential Study in Sanity and Madness.* Harmondsworth: Penguin, Pelican Books, 1965.

Lee, Harold N. "Mead's Doctrine of the Past." *Tulane Studies in Philosophy* 12 (1963):52–75.

Marcuse, Herbert. *Eros and Civilization—A Philosophical Inquiry into Freud.* Boston: Beacon Press, 1955. Paperback, with new preface: New York: Random House, Vintage Books, 1962.

———. *One-Dimensional Man: Studies in the Ideology of Advanced Industrial Society.* Boston: Beacon Press, 1964.

———. "Sartre's Existentialism." In *Studies in Critical Philosophy,* pp. 157–90. London: New Left Books, 1972. Reprint, Boston: Beacon Press, 1973. First appeared without postscript as "Existentialism: Remarks on Jean-Paul Sartre's *L'Être et le Néant.*" *Philosophy and Phenomenological Research* 8 (March 1948):309–36.

Marx, Karl. *Capital,* vol. 1. Edited by Frederick Engels. New York: International Publishers, 1967.

———. "Economic and Philosophical Manuscripts of 1844." In *Karl Marx, Frederick Engels, Collected Works,* vol. 3, pp. 229–346. London: Lawrence & Wishart; New York: International Publishers; Moscow: Progress Publishers, 1975.

May, Rollo; Angel, Ernest; and Ellenberger, Henri F., ed. *Existence: A*

New Dimension in Psychiatry and Psychology. New York: Basic Books, 1958. Reprint, New York: Simon and Schuster, Clarion Books, 1958.

Mead, George Herbert. "The Genesis of the Self and Social Control." *International Journal of Ethics* 35 (1924–25):251–77. Reprinted in *Selected Writings,* edited by Andrew J. Reck, pp. 267–93. Chicago: University of Chicago Press, Phoenix Edition, 1981.

————. "The Mechanism of Social Consciousness." *Journal of Philosophy* 9 (1912):401–06. Reprinted in *Selected Writings,* edited by Andrew J. Reck, pp. 134–41. Chicago: University of Chicago Press, Phoenix Edition, 1981.

————. *Mind, Self, and Society: From the Standpoint of a Social Behaviorist.* Edited, with an introduction, by Charles W. Morris. Chicago: University of Chicago Press, 1934.

————. *Movements of Thought in the Nineteenth Century.* Edited, with an introduction, by Merritt H. Moore. Chicago: University of Chicago Press, 1936.

————. *Philosophy of the Act.* Edited, with an introduction, by Charles W. Morris in collaboration with John M. Brewster, Albert M. Dunham, and David L. Miller. Chicago: University of Chicago Press, 1938.

————. *The Philosophy of the Present.* Edited, with an introduction, by Arthur E. Murphy. Prefatory remarks by John Dewey. Chicago: Open Court, 1932. Reprint, Chicago: University of Chicago Press, Phoenix Edition, 1980.

————. "The Social Self." *Journal of Philosophy* 10 (1913):374–80. Reprinted in *Selected Writings,* edited by Andrew J. Reck, pp. 142–49. Chicago: University of Chicago Press, Phoenix Edition, 1981.

Miller, David L. *George Herbert Mead: Self, Language, and the World.* Austin: University of Texas Press, 1973. Reprint, Chicago: University of Chicago Press, Phoenix Edition, 1980.

Natanson, Maurice. *The Social Dynamics of George H. Mead.* Introduction by Horace M. Kallen. Washington, D.C.: Public Affairs Press, 1956.

Nietzsche, Friedrich. *Beyond Good and Evil.* In *Basic Writings of Nietzsche,* translated by Walter Kaufmann. New York: Random House, Modern Library, 1966.

————. *Thus Spoke Zarathustra.* In *The Portable Nietzsche,* translated by Walter Kaufmann. Canada: Macmillan; New York: Viking Press, 1954.

————. *Twilight of the Idols.* In *The Portable Nietzsche,* translated by Walter Kaufmann. Canada: Macmillan; New York: Viking Press, 1954.

Pfuetze, Paul E. *The Social Self.* New York: Bookman Associates, 1954. Revised and reprinted as *Self, Society, Existence: Human Nature and Dialogue in the Thought of George Herbert Mead and Martin Buber.* New York: Harper and Row, Torchbooks, 1961.

Plato. *Symposium*. In *Great Dialogues of Plato,* translated by W. H. D. Rouse; edited by Eric H. Warmington and Philip G. Rouse, pp. 69–117. New York: New American Library, Mentor Books, 1956.

Reck, Andrew J. "The Philosophy of George Herbert Mead (1863–1931)." *Tulane Studies in Philosophy* 12 (1963):5–51.

———, ed. *Selected Writings: George Herbert Mead.* With an introduction by Reck. Indianapolis: Bobbs-Merrill, Library of Liberal Arts, 1964. Reprint, Chicago: University of Chicago Press, Phoenix Edition, 1981.

Sartre, Jean-Paul. *Being and Nothingness: An Essay on Phenomenological Ontology.* Translated, with an introduction, by Hazel E. Barnes. New York: Philosophical Library, 1956.

———. *Nausea.* Translated by Lloyd Alexander. New York: New Directions, 1949.

———. *The Transcendence of the Ego.* Translated by Forrest Williams and Robert Kirkpatrick. New York: Noonday Press, 1957.

——— and Fretz, Leo. "An Interview with Jean-Paul Sartre." In *Jean-Paul Sartre—Contemporary Approaches to His Philosophy,* edited by Hugh J. Silverman and Frederick A. Elliston, pp. 221–39. Pittsburgh: Duquesne University Press, 1980.

———; Gruenheck, Susan; Pucciani, Oreste F.; and Rybalka, Michel. "An Interview with Jean-Paul Sartre." In *The Philosophy of Jean-Paul Sartre, Library of Living Philosophers, Vol. XVI,* edited by Paul Arthur Schilpp, pp. 5–51. La Salle, Illinois: Open Court, 1981.

Schuetz, Alfred. "Sartre's Theory of the Alter Ego." *Philosophy and Phenomenological Research* 9 (December 1948):181–99. Reprinted in *Collected Papers,* vol. I, edited by M. Natanson, pp. 180–203. The Hague: Martinus Nijhoff, 1962.

Spinoza, Benedict de. *Ethics.* Translated by W. H. White and A. H. Sterling. Edited, with an introduction, by James Gutmann. New York: Hafner, 1949.

Stone, Gregory P., and Farberman, Harvey A. *Social Psychology Through Symbolic Interaction.* Waltham: Ginn, 1970.

Index

Act, 5, 17; social, 82
Anticipation, 64, 96; defined, 97–98; world of, 66, 99

Bad faith, 45, 46, 100, 114
Behavior: impulsive, 83*n*11; purposeful, 25; reinforcement of, 103; specific, 56
Being-for-others, 36, 40–44, 47–51, 48*n*, 90–91
Being-for-self, 110–12
Body: and self, 78, 80. *See also* Limit; Other
Buber, Martin, 115*n*

Choice, 59–60, 68; before consciously determined, 92; existential, xiii, xiv; and freedom, xv, 124, 125; self-conscious, 58, 68; and sense of self, 74; subject capable of, 69
Cogito, 44, 45, 48*n*, 51*n*
Conflict, 91; generated by prohibitions, 81–82; and the negative, 86; no and impulse, 88–89; psychological repercussions of, 82; resolution of, 17, 88*n*; self and other, 107. *See also* Consciousness; Mead; No
Consciousness, xv, 45; adult, 107; anticipatory, 97; bifurcation of, 64–65, 65*n*; birth of, 73; birth

of, for Sartre, 33–35; can only limit itself, 48, 90; and conflict, 83–84; as detotalized totality, 31; as ekstatic, 29–30, 59; emergence of, 34; freedom of, 51–52; human, 49; mediating self and not-self, 98; nature of, for Sartre, 28–31; negation of itself, 61; negative in, 84–89; nihilation of itself, 30–31; nihilations of, 60–61; non-positional, 36; not purely spontaneous, 61; as observer and observed, 22–23; ontological nature of, 33; personal, 97; positional, 36; radically free, 31; spontaneous, 31, 34, 35, 38, 60, 68, 90; stream of, 23, 32, 57, 99; as unified and dispersed, 31; unity of, 61; uses of term for Mead, 8. *See also* Freedom; Future; Lack; Non-reflective; Nothing; Not-self; Novel; Past; Possibilities; Presence; Present; Role; Sense of self; Temporal
Contingency, 34, 62, 62*n*12
Contradiction: felt, 84, 91; Hegel on, 84

Dependence: on the other, 103, 106, 108; of slave, 114

Determinism: "I" rescues us from, 25; Mead's refutation of, 15–17; science route of, 46; without nothing there is, 47

Development. *See* Mind; Object-self; Reflective consciousness; Self; Self-consciousness; Sense of self

Ego: aware of itself, 9, 58; constituted by consciousness, 35; emergence of, 35; Freud on the, 85–88, 85*n*; not behind consciousness, 35, 38; not personalizing pole, 37, 59; as quasi-object, 35; transcendental, 99; as transcendent phenomenon, 59. *See also* Self; Superego

Ego ideal. *See* Superego

Emergence, 6, 21, 62*n*1; of mind, 8. *See also* Mead

Experience: contact, 79; includes immediate for Mead, 4; of infant, 73–74; non-reflective, 3, 73; pre-reflective, xiv, 56, 73; push and pull of, 17; reflective, 56

For-itself, 108; birth of, 33–35; defined, 28; ontological structure of, 39, 48*n*, 49; as temporal, 30; transformed into object, 47–48

Freedom, xvi; anguish over, 65; awareness of, 59–60; of consciousness, 35, 41, 46, 51–52; defined, 58, 124; degrees of, 66; depends on the other, 105; hinges on nothing, 34; loss of, 39; negative, 49; as not being determined, 66; in *Philosophy of the Act*, 66–67; pre-reflective key to, 58; presence of, 115*n*; for Sartre, 67–68, 114; sense of, given by "I," 14; sociology of xiii, xv; source of, 25; stolen 42, 54. *See also* Choice; Nothing; Perspective; Self-determination

Free will: and self-determination, 100; and soul, 125

Freud, Sigmund: on aggression 119–23. *See also* Ego; Identification; Instinct; Superego

Functional identity, 7

Future: and consciousness, 37, 68, 99; hypothetical, 63, 83*n*11; independence of, 83; of one's own, 117–18; orientation toward, 64; and past, 124; and present, 20. *See also* Mead; Not-self

Games: organized, 9; rules of, 10, 10*n*

Generalized other: and communities, 12*n*; defined, 10; internalization of, 21; and "me," 20–21; and object-self, 80; and recognition, 116–17, 119; and self, 10–11; self mirrors, 21; taking the role of the, 11–12, 15. *See also* Perspective

Gestures: conscious or unconscious, 7; conversation of, 5, 7; defined, 5; and thinking, 11*n*. *See also* Mind; Significant symbol; Verbal (Vocal) gesture

Hegel, G. W. F., 4; on contingency, 20*n*; on contradiction, 84; on limit, xiv, 75–78, 88–89; master–slave dialectic, xiv, 41, 41*n*, 105–15; on nature, 62, 62*n*12; on time, 29–31, 60–61; systemic universe of, 62; when read by Sartre, 41*n*

"I": ambiguity in Mead's view of, 25; calls out me, 17; cannot be aware of itself, 53; creative activities of, 25; defined, 13–15; as fiction, 56–57; functional, 13, 17, 25; initiates action and novel responses, 14; introduction of, 80; necessary presupposition, 56–57; needs self for reflection, 58; not solely functional distinction, 25, 57; as noumenal phantom, 26; as observer, 38; pole, 15; and running current of awareness, 22–23, 53–55; spontaneity of, 12, 13, 25–26, 54, 67. *See also* "Me"; Personality

Identification, xiv, xv, 82, 82n, 121

Impulse, 81–82, 94, 120; defined, 122; gratification of, 93; Mead's definition of, 81n; as not-self, 88; remaining with, 89. *See also* Instinct; Prohibitions

Independence: desire for, 107–10; of humanized object, 111; master does not have, 113–14; promotion of, 118; of worker, 111

In-itself: and consciousness, 31, 32, 34, 48; defined, 28; nihilation of, 34; unity of, 108

Instinct, 124, 125; of death, 120, 121; Freud on, 121n; frustration of, 121; of love, 120, 121. *See also* Impulse

Internalization, 82, 122; of the other, 21, 43, 50, 52. *See also* Generalized other; Negation; No; Prohibitions

James, William, 83

Kant, Immanuel: on person, 104

Lack, xvi; and activity, 96; awareness of, 78; and consciousness, 59–60, 65; experience of, 95; and limit, 78; negation of, 61, 96; as overcome, 101; personal, 105; and pre-reflective consciousness, 95–101; and self-determination, 98; and selfness, 37, 59. *See also* Not-self; Perspective; Sense of self

Language, 6, 7; sign, 6n6

Limit, xiv, 96; awareness of, 100; of awareness, 59, 97; and the body, 78; development of consciousness of, 94–95; develop-

ment of self, 75; dialectic of, 75–78, 88–89; ideal, 78, 98; me-as-object as, 41, 47–48; mediation of, 76; negative as, 105; and object-self, 111–12; of pre-reflective consciousness, 37, 68; qualitative, 75–76, 88, 91, 111–12; of self, 100; self aware of, 75; self as, of awareness, 37; and sense of self, 78; understood in terms of negation, 81. *See also* Consciousness; Lack; No; Not-self

Look, the, 51, 52, 66; alternative to Sartre's account of, 54–56; object-self and, 90–91; Sartre on, 38–44, 126; Sartre's account critiqued, 48–52. *See also* Pre-reflective consciousness

Market economy, xvi, 125

Marx, Karl, 105; on imagination, 17n

Master–Slave dialectic, xiv, 41, 41n, 105–15; and recognition, 112–15

"Me":as commenting, 23; conservative, 61; defined, 13–15; empirical self, 13; functional, 13, 17, 25; and generalized other, 20–21; has latent existence, 15; not solely functional distinction, 25, 57; novel happens to, 58; as object, 13, 22; organized set of attitudes, 14; reorganization of, 17; and running current of awareness, 22–23, 53–55; system, 21, 57, 65, 100. *See also* "I"; Personality; Self

Mead, George Herbert, xiv, 3, 45; behaviorism of, 4–5; on conflict, 81–84; cosmopolitanism, 13; on determinism, 15–17; John Dewey on, 3; on emergence, 18–22; as empirical scientist, 25; future for, 64n–65n; and Hegel, 20n; on individual, 12, 13;

Mead, George Herbert (*continued*)
metaphysical implications of position, 62–63; as metaphysician,
25; on objectivity, 19n20; on
physical things, 78–80; pragmatist, 4; on reflection, 33, 52–53;
on systemic change, 18–22; on
values, 24
Meaning: defined, 6n5, 7
Mediated: being, 115; natural is,
110, 113; self, 103; self defined,
xvi
Mediating: consciousness, self and
not-self, 98; self, 103; self defined, xvi
Mind, 50; development of, 3, 8;
function of, 64n–65n; importance of gesture for, 5; and significant symbol, 8; social phenomenon, 8

Negation: and aggression compared, 122; internalized, 92,
122; of the negation, 29, 77–78;
and object-self, 81, 109. *See also*
Limit; Not-self; Otherness
Negative: in consciousness, 84–89;
as prohibition, 91–92; and self-
determination, 93; and sociality,
95; and work, 110–12
No: child's use of, 107; and conflict, 86; as deformed limit, 123;
feeling the, 84; infant's use of,
74; internalization of, 85–89,
100, 101; as limit, 85; and object-self, 88; of the other, 111,
122–23; pervasive quality of,
91; power of the, 104; as prohibition, 82; recognition of child's,
118–19, 123–24; and sense of
self, 74; use against the other,
112; uses of, 94; as verbal gesture, 87–88, 92, 93, 95, 109,
122–23
Non-reflective: consciousness, 45,
54, 64; experience, 3, 4, 53, 73
Nothing: consciousness as, 28–30,

34, 41, 46, 60–61, 77, 91–92,
96; consciousness cannot be,
49–50; and freedom, 47; this,
48
Not-self, 84, 123; and consciousness, 95–101, 96n; defined, 97;
and future, 95, 97; and lack,
97–98; as limit, 110; negation
of, 60–61, 96n, 100, 105, 111;
and object-self, 105; presence of,
99; as there, 98
Novel, 57; absolutely, 62; event as
transitional, 19; events, xvi; experiences and consciousness, 65–
66; history requires the, 63; initiated by "I," 14–15; in social-
psychological terms, 63; transforms past, 22. *See also* Reflection
Novelty, 50; change and, 67; degrees of, 14–15; and object-self,
99; and self, 57–58; and sense
of self, 94–95; and stability, 18;
status of, 63; universe contains,
15–17, 25

Object: beings-as, 40, 47; defined,
29n; experience of being, 38;
nihilation of the, 48–49; to oneself, 55, 73, 74, 79; for the
other, 41, 55; other converted
into, 40–41; pre-reflective
awareness of, 31–32. *See also*
Object-self; Other; Self
Object-self, 11, 38–39, 47, 53–54,
64, 69, 74, 75, 89; circumscribed, 123, 125–26; cognition
and, 116; comfortable, 105;
content of, 103; delimit one as,
104; development of, 85, 93–
94, 106–12, 115–19; development of self arrested at, 114–19;
as here, 98; indirect presence of,
99; is mediated being, 115; me-
as-object compared to, 91; as
me-system, 21; and the non-
conscious, 124; precedes sense

of self, 81; and recognition, 115–19; as relational system, 100; and temporality, 83; as totality, 57. *See also* Generalized other; Limit; Look; Negation; Not-self; Novelty

Other, the, 47, 50, 96, 121; and the body, 78; as caretaker, 103; child's impact on, 123–24; differentiation from, 48; empirical presence of, 42–43, 54; fear of, 87; and for-itself, 48; freedom depends on, 105; interiorized on reflective level, 43*n*–44*n*, 52; keeping at bay, 48; mediation of, 42; non-being of, 76–77, 88–89; non-empirical, 43–44, 50–52, 55–56; as object, 40–43; object for, 39; separation from, 40; taking the attitude of, 8, 10–11; taking the response of, 82; taking the role of, 9–10, 13, 15, 16–17, 21, 43, 46, 54–55, 61, 64, 74, 92, 116, 121. *See also* Dependence; Freedom; Generalized other; Internalization; Otherness; Perspective; Presence

Otherness, 32, 84, 86, 88; negation of, 106–13; of the other, 49

Past: of consciousness, 98–99; of for-itself, 33–34; and future, 124; hypothetical, 63, 83*n*11; independence of, 83; and present, 19; rejecting of, 57–58; transformed by novel, 22

Personality, 57; phases of, 18; as unity of "I" and "me," 17–18, 18*n*, 20–22; whole, 66–67

Perspective: and freedom, 16–17; of the generalized other, 11, 46, 56, 116; and lack, 65; new, 17; of the other, 8, 11, 46, 54, 63–64, 74, 116; and system, 63

Play: importance of, 8–9

Possibilities: anticipate, 64; and consciousness, xvi, 37, 39*n*, 59–60, 68, 74, 75; organization of my, 39

Pre-reflective consciousness, xiv, 68; and anticipation, 64; cannot be its own object, 43; as impersonal, 36; insecurity of, 73; of the look, 50; as personal, 37; self of, 39, 53, 56, 58–59; self-consciousness, 36–38, 52, 65*n*; and sociality 63–64; teleological dimension of, 96. *See also* Experience; Lack; Presence; Reflective consciousness

Presence: in absence, 42, 47, 51; to all men, 50; of consciousness, 59–60; original, 43; of the other, 51; and pre-reflective consciousness, 37

Present: of consciousness, 98–99; eternal, 20; and future, 20; immediate, 83–84; independence of, 83; as negation of itself, 29–30; and past, 19; reality is in, 63; specious, 64*n*, 83, 83*n*

Prohibitions, 81–82, 102, 107; converted to ego ideal, 87; as ideals, 122; and impulses, 84–88; internalization of, 84, 91, 93; negative and, 91–92. *See also* No

Psychology: introspective, 5, 45; and limit, 88; modern, xiii; Sartre on, 27–28; sciences of, 46

Recognition, xv, 49; authentic, 113; of autonomy, 104; caretaker's, 117; and master–slave dialectic, 112–15; mutual, 118, 125–26; peer, 113, 117; primordial refusal of, 118; pseudo, 114–17; of self-consciousness, 107–09, 116; and sense of self, 112, 117–19. *See also* Generalized other; No; Object-self

Reflection: act of, 24; for adult,
98–99; and arrest of spontaneity, 31, 34, 35; and change, 67;
extended present of, 83; "I" and
"me" required for, 65; impure,
31–33, 31n, 35, 57; and the
novel, 66; and otherness, 32;
pure, 31–33; as reasoning, 4;
self of, 10, 36; as self-
consciousness, 3–4; and self-
determination, 100–01; and
sense of self, 95. See also "I";
Mead
Reflective consciousness, xiv, xvi,
44n, 56; development of, 8, 73;
and pre-reflective consciousness,
xvi, 31–33
Role: complex set of responses, 8–
9; conceptualization of, 81; consciousness of, 46; of parent, 82,
92; playing, 21; Sartre on, 28–
29; and self, 11; separated temporally from other roles, 82–83
Role-taking, 47, 52, 95; and physical things, 79–80. See also Generalized other; Other
Royce, Josiah, 4

Sartre: xiv, 45; existentialism of,
xiv, 4; on metaphysical questions, 33–34; on philosophy, 3,
27–28; on psychology, 27–28.
See also Consciousness; Freedom; Hegel; Role; Self
Self, xiii; begins as behaviors, 11;
as bounded, 74; and cognitive
knowledge, 38; complexity of,
11; constituted by consciousness, 35; constituted by interiorized other, 43n–44n; development of, xv, xvii, 3, 54, 75,
114–19; essence is cognitive,
11n; future, 64; as ideal, 37, 39,
59; indirect awareness of, 32,
36, 53, 58; knowledge of, 24–
25; and "me," 18n; in memory,
24; as me-system, 21; new, 118;

as object, xiv, 32, 33, 36–38,
41, 45, 56, 61, 67–68; object of
cognition, 36, 64, 65, 68, 80; as
object not free, 57–58; as open
system, 68; reconstructed, 67;
requires self-consciousness, 10,
11n, 24; and sociality, 68; social
nature of, 11; as story, 67–68;
as system, xvi, 21, 63; true, is
cognitive, 45; unity of, 10–11;
use in ch. 4, 74; use in ch. 5,
102n; and values, 24; as whole,
56, 67; and work, 96n. See also
Body; Generalized other; Limit;
Mediated; Mediating; Novelty;
Pre-reflective consciousness; Psychology; Reflection; Role; Self-
consciousness
Self-consciousness, xv; alienation
of, 108; as awareness of meaning, 7; desire of, 106–10; development of, 3, 69, 106–09; and
group attitudes, 12; non-thetic,
39n. See also Pre-reflective consciousness; Recognition; Self;
Significant symbol; Temporal
Self-determination, xiii–xiv, 27,
63, 81, 126; defined, xv, xvi, 58,
68, 100–01; and freedom, 104–
05; self-conscious, 67–69; and
social, xv. See also Free will;
Lack; Negative; Reflection;
Sense of self
Selfness, 47; circuit of, 39n, 41;
defined, 36–38, 97–98; and
lack, 37, 59; not, 40–41, 47. See
also Sense of self
Sense of self, 68, 103, 124, 126;
and bad faith, 114; and consciousness, 59–60; development
of, 73–74, 92–101; illusory, 57;
and lack, 85; and master–slave
dialectic, 110–12; non-
cognitive, 37–38; not prior to
reflection, 65; is pre-reflective,
37–38; and self-determination,
xv, 102–03; and sociality, 85;

synonymous with selfness, 37. *See also* Limit; No; Novelty; Recognition; Selfness

Significant symbol: defined, 5–6; and self-consciousness, 7; vocal gesture as, 6–7. *See also* Gesture; Mind; Verbal (Vocal) gesture

Sociality, xvi, 57, 61, 84, 98, 100; and change in the "me," 21; and the child, 94–95; defined, 18–20; habituated to, 110. *See also* Negative; Pre-reflective consciousness; Self

Solipsism, 42–44, 49–51

Spinoza, xv, 62, 90, 92

Spontaneity, xiv, 66, 25; arrested, 39. *See also* Consciousness

Subject: free, 69; and object dichotomy, 9–10, 56, 99; seer of object, 39

Superego, 43n16, 82, 85–88, 86n–87n, 123; derivation of, 120–21

Symbolic interaction, xv, 3, 44

System, 18–22; alteration of, 99–100; closed, 16, 63–64; family as, 10; independence of, 20n; new, 94; old and new, 19–22, 57, 61–62; as organized set of responses, 10; pond as, 18; socioeconomic, xvi, xvii; totalizing, 62. *See also* Mead; Perspective; Self

Temporal, consciousness as, 29–30, 33, 46, 59, 64; disjunction, 82; experience of the, 83; nature of reality, 15; and self-consciousness, 9. *See also* Object-self

Time: dependent on the novel, 16; and negativity, 29–31. *See also* Hegel; Role

Unconscious, 24; gestures, 7; inimical to freedom, 124; unnecessary for unity of consciousness, 59

Verbal (Vocal) gesture, 52; defined, 6; implicit response to, 8; and response, 53–55. *See also* Gesture; No; Significant symbol

Work. *See* Negative; Self

World that is there, 4, 23, 45